Whether it is popular or biblical, a proverb conveys profound wisdom in pithy terms and a succinct, memorable form. King Solomon is reputed to have produced 3,000 of these sayings, and much of his work has been preserved for all time in the Book of Proverbs.

D. Stuart Briscoe takes Solomon's ancient wisdom and applies it to the problems we all face today, providing sound sense for successful living in a thoroughly scriptural manner. The wisdom of the ages is available and workable for you — no matter how modern your problems.

Sound Sense
for
Successful Living

D. Stuart Briscoe

SPIRE BOOKS

Fleming H. Revell Company
Old Tappan, N.J.

ISBN 0-8007-8410-3
A Spire Book
Published by Fleming H. Revell Company
Original edition published
by Ideals Publishing Corporation
under the title
Sound Sense for Successful Living.

Contents

Contents

Sound Sense
for
Successful Living

ONE

The Beginning of Wisdom

The fear of the LORD is the beginning of wisdom, and knowledge of the Holy One is understanding.

Proverbs 9:10

I have a tendency to procrastinate. From my earliest years I have seldom done today what I can leave till tomorrow. My math teacher in high school was aware of my problem and wrote in my autograph book, "Do it now"—advice as superb as it is succinct. As a small boy I ripped my pants but was most reluctant to interrupt my busy life so that my mother could do the necessary repairs. She prevailed upon me to submit to her needle saying as she sewed, "A stitch in time saves nine."

It would be wrong of me to suggest that I fully understood what she was saying, but I certainly got the drift. The words she spoke had an unusual quality, a penetrating brevity that not only registered in my young mind but actually stayed there. Down through the years filled with procrastinating moments and delayed actions, my mother's words have reverberated through my reluctant consciousness and quite often I have acted upon them!

A proverb, for I subsequently discovered that was what my mother had quoted, is intended to convey profound wisdom in pithy terms and succinct arresting form. Nobody knows who first used the proverb, but there is ample evidence that the Chinese, the Indians, the Sumerians, the Greeks, the Romans, and the Hebrews were skilled in its use. In fact, some of the modern proverbs like, "A bird in the hand is worth two in the bush" first saw the light of day in the Middle Ages and, "Forewarned is forearmed" started out a *Praemonitus Praemunitis* in Roman times.

In more recent times Ben Franklin used proverbs to get his opinions on life in colonial America across to the settlers. When he wasn't inventing stoves or experimenting with kites, writing Declarations of Independence or advancing theories of atmospherics, he was playing chess, visiting France, opening fire departments, libraries, or universities, and publishing *Poor Richard's Almanac.* This annual publication, full of wise sayings culled from Europe and prepared for American consumption, was widely acclaimed.

It is doubtful, however, if even the popularity of Benjamin Franklin's proverbs approached the popularity of King Solomon's wise sayings. He certainly outstripped his contemporaries in the East, and such was his fame that people came from the surrounding nations to drink at the fountain of his wisdom and carry it away in the convenient receptacles of his proverbs. He is reputed to have produced three thousand proverbs as well as a thousand-and-five songs, and much of his work has been preserved for all generations in the Old Testament book entitled, "Proverbs."

The most famous of the visiting dignitaries whom Solomon entertained was undoubtedly the legendary Queen of Sheba, who journeyed over 1,200 miles from what is now called Yemen to meet him. She was skeptical of the reports that she heard in her native land of the wisdom and wealth of Solomon, so she decided to go and see for herself. The preparations she made and the pomp and circumstance with which she arrived suggest that she might have been more interested in displaying her wealth and splendor than discovering Solomon's, and the determination with which she set about him with "hard questions" indicated her desire to expose the limits of his knowledge and explode the myth of his magnificence.

But her plans were thwarted and she graciously admitted that all she had heard about Solomon was true and, in fact, she had not been told half the truth. She was so overwhelmed by him that she gave him over four tons of gold and more spices than he could use in a lifetime. Before she packed her belongings and boarded her camel for home, she said almost wistfully, "How happy your men must be! How happy your officials, who continually stand before you and hear your wisdom! Praise be to the LORD your God who has delighted in you and placed you on the throne of Israel. Because of the LORD'S eternal love for Israel, he has made you king, to maintain justice and righteousness" (1 Kings 10:8, 9). For the Queen of Sheba to speak in such glowing terms of Jehovah (for that is the true meaning of the word translated "LORD") is remarkable when we remember that her people engaged in polytheistic worship of sun, moon, and stars.

Solomon had been careful to point out that his wisdom was a result of his relationship with Jehovah. He related to the Queen a most remarkable experience he had in Gibeon when he was a young man. One night he dreamed that the Lord had offered him anything he wished and he had replied, "You have made your servant King in place of my father, David. But I am only a little child. . . . So give your servant a discerning heart to govern your people and to distinguish between right and wrong" (1 Kings 3:7–9). Knowing the sort of things that people usually ask for in such circumstances, the Lord was so delighted with Solomon's request that He not only granted it but gave him all kinds of things for which he didn't ask. There was no doubt, therefore, in Solomon's mind that his wisdom was a gift from the Lord. Evidently in his talks with the Queen of Sheba he had been able to convince her of the truthfulness of this story, because she did not hesitate to thank Solomon and also praise the Lord.

If the "Proverbs" are to be read so as to derive the utmost benefit, it is necessary that they should be seen as more than just a collection of pithy sayings from antiquity along with all the other relics of ancient wisdom. They should be recognized as being a special revelation of the mind of Jehovah made known through inspiration to his servant Solomon.

The Scriptures have many references to the inspiring work of God. Isaiah, writing some two hundred years after Solomon, expressed sentiments not dissimilar to those of the wise King. Speaking prophetically of the Branch who should come and exercise his ministry so effectively that "the nations will rally to him" he said, "The Spirit of the LORD will rest upon him—the Spirit of wisdom and understanding, the Spirit of counsel and of power, the Spirit of knowledge and the fear of the LORD, and he will delight in the fear of the LORD" (Isaiah 11:2, 3).

The similarities between the wisdom and understanding that both Solomon and "the Branch" enjoyed through the work of the Spirit of the Lord in their lives is obvious and it is interesting to note that James called it, "the wisdom that comes from heaven" and described it as "first of all pure; then peace-loving, considerate, submissive, full of mercy and good fruit, impartial and sincere."

There is, therefore, a vastly important added dimension to the Proverbs of Scripture. All proverbs contain an earthy and practical wisdom, but these Proverbs claim to originate with the Lord and, accordingly, project a heavenly and eternal dimension. In addition to being immensely practical, they are intensely spiritual and should be read with this in mind. There are certain similarities between Solomon's proverbs and those of other people who claim no heavenly enlightenment. In fact, some of Solomon's work is very closely related to that of his contemporaries and some of his proverbs may even have been borrowed from other sources. This does not negate the claim to inspiration, but rather demonstrates the fact that God reveals his truth in many ways to many people, because truth wherever found is always God's truth.

Solomon wasted no time getting to the point. Having briefly outlined the purpose of Proverbs, he stated bluntly, "The fear of the LORD is the beginning of knowledge" (Proverbs 1:7). His unequivocal statement sets the tone for everything that follows and should not be overlooked. To many people God is an afterthought. When they get into trouble over their heads they struggle and shout until as a last resort, they try God. This becomes increasingly clear to me in my pastoral ministry. Every week I meet people whose lives resemble a disaster area. They have often contributed to the disaster over a long period of time, and only when it became apparent to them that matters were out of their control, have they looked around for help. But many times they look only to man. They turn to the agencies, the government or the experts in various fields to solve their problems and banish their dilemmas, and in my experience only after they have exhausted all other avenues do they turn to the Lord. In other words, the Lord is last hope. Some people have even told me,

"I've tried everything and it didn't work, so now I'll try religion and if this doesn't work, I've no alternative but to end it all."

Solomon would have taken issue with this attitude as his opening statement clearly demonstrates. The Lord is not the final stopping place in the frantic search for answers. He is the starting place which alone can help us know the right questions. A pastor-friend of mine tried to persuade me to move to California as he thought that was the best place for a ministry in the United States. When I asked him how he had arrived at that conclusion he answered semi-facetiously, "So many people think that California holds all the answers to their dilemmas. Sunny skies, warm temperatures, beaches for lazing on, mountains for skiing down, casual life-styles, glamorous people, and plenty of money. But when they have been here a little while, the Utopia begins to develop cracks and they become disillusioned. Previously, when they were disillusioned they moved farther west, but having arrived in California the only place west is the Pacific. They consider the Pacific and draw back from that solution and at that point remember the pastor. California is the place to be!" He didn't convince me that I should move west, but he did illustrate the contemporary mentality that so often relegates spiritual answers to last place on the list of solutions to earth's problems.

Perhaps man's greatest problem arises from the fact that he has been remarkably successful in many areas. He has learned to combat many diseases, to control his environment, to predict his behavior, to settle disputes and resolve many seemingly intractable problems. He has become so blinded by his dazzling array of trophies that he has overlooked the fact that for every solution he has found, ten problems remain unresolved. This pride in achievement and myopia towards lack of achievement have led man to adopt an almost divine posture, and his popular wisdom is, "the reverence of man is the beginning of wisdom." But this attitude must be discarded not only because it contradicts Scripture, but also because it elevates man to a position his record does not merit and lays upon him a burden his obvious weakness cannot bear. For all the victories man has won, for which we are all immeasurably grateful, death, disease, hatred, bloodshed, malice, greed and innumerable evidences of "man's inhumanity to man" continue to abound. Any philosophy that starts with man must end with man and live with man's weakness and be limited to man's abilities. This damns the human race to a world which man himself has constructed which may yet destroy him; but much worse, it denies him anything beyond the grave. If man is the sum and circumference of his own being, this life is all there is. A dismal and discouraging thought!

Solomon knew better. He did not start and finish with man, he started and finished with the Lord. To him man was not a chance accident thrown up on the shores of a tiny planet to exist in the vastness of an unfathomable universe. Solomon believed that behind all things stood the Self-Existent One who, without beginning or end, needed nothing or no person to survive. This One, Jehovah the Lord, designed and brought into being all things that do exist and, therefore, in him and in him alone lay the secret of existence and the meaning of being. In a similar passage to the one we have been considering, Solomon added, "The fear of the LORD is the beginning of wisdom, and knowledge of the Holy One is understanding" (Proverbs 9:10).

To understand his existence or to fathom her being, a man or woman needs to start with the Lord who made them for a purpose. Failure to start with "knowledge of the Holy One" will no more produce the correct answers than running the ball in the wrong direction will produce a winning score.

There is another aspect to this approach to wisdom and understanding. The Lord is to be rightly regarded. It is "the fear of the LORD" that counts. This does not mean that we should be terrified of God but it does mean that we should reverence him as supreme and submit to him as Master and Lord. There are plenty of people who "believe in God," but demonstrate by attitude and life-style a total disregard for his wishes and complete disdain for his commands. The God in whom they believe is shown by such behavior to be a god other than the One of whom Solomon spoke. When he is rightly known, he is fully reverenced, and a humble, submissive spirit in daily living is the evidence of such a relationship.

The common misconception that the Lord can be

known and trusted and life-styles contrary to him maintained is clearly denied by the definition, "To fear the Lord is to hate evil." In case there should be any debate about what constitutes evil, he added, "I hate pride and arrogance, evil behavior and perverse speech." Nothing is more intrinsically evil in God's eyes than the attitude of a man's heart that establishes himself in God's position and runs his own affairs without due recognition of God's sole right to be God. This is the pride and the arrogance of which he speaks, and the resultant behavior and speech understandably are classified as "evil" and "perverse."

With telling bluntness the writer of Proverbs described those who deny the Lord both in life and speech as "fools" and claimed that they "despise wisdom and discipline." Strong words indeed but necessary, for if the fear of the Lord is indeed the beginning of wisdom then some of those brilliant people who are basking in the sunshine of academic acclaim may be "fools" and others who never claimed academic excellence but believed they were running their lives adequately may be running them adequately in the wrong direction. Paul expressed these solemn thoughts powerfully. He said, "Although they claimed to be wise, they became fools . . . " (Romans 1:22), and on another occasion he wrote of those who were "always learning but never able to acknowledge the truth . . . " (2 Timothy 3:7). These remarks of Solomon and Paul should not, of course, be regarded as anti-intellectual, for both men demonstrated that they were remarkably gifted and scholarly men. They should be seen as clear statements that all knowledge gained must be applied to living a life that acknowledges the Lord as Lord and sees in him the only integrating point of reality and the measure of truth.

TWO

Everything You Wanted to Know About Knowledge

*Whoever loves discipline loves knowledge,
but he who hates correction is stupid.*

Proverbs 12:1

Life in the old quarter of the city of Jerusalem is, to a Westerner, a tumult of color, movement, conversation, smell, and sound. The narrow streets, lined with small stores whose wares seem to encroach on the already limited space reserved for travel, are jammed with people jostling and gesticulating. I love to wander slowly past the piles of merchandise, sometimes allowing the insistent salesmen to maneuver me into their place of business to examine piles of sticky confections, stacks of brightly colored materials, watches, cameras, exquisite copperware, camel saddles and curios. With remarkable tenacity, yet with rare good humor, they barter and bargain, earnest faces ever ready to break into wrinkled grins when their "bargains" are shown to be something considerably less. There is, however, one major problem with this kind of activity. You can get hopelessly lost in the maze, and this I did on one memorable occasion.

A small boy with quick eyes saw my hesitation and pulling on my arm said, "You lost Mister? I get you to your hotel." He was one of the masses of youngsters who wriggle and squirm their way through the impassable crowds, drawing people into stores with promises of unspeakable opportunities, selling packs of chewing gum or carved olive wood necklaces always "two for a dollar," and as far as I can see generally keeping old Jerusalem economically viable.

"Where you wish to go?" he inquired.

"I want to find the group I'm leading," I replied.

Amusement flitting across his bright face, he asked with just the right touch of irony, "You the leader? Who your guide?"

"Sari Rabadi," I replied, giving the name of the Bedouin Christian who was enriching our tour with his remarkable insights into the Holy Land.

"I know Sari," he said, puffing out his cheeks and sticking out his small stomach in a comical imitation of Sari's ample proportions. "Come with me," he added and without more ado, he plunged into the crowds, pulling me by the wrist.

The next few minutes were a continual source of amazement to me. The boy, whose age I could not estimate with any degree of certainty, talked incessantly about America, assuming by my appearance that I came from that country. Yet he was astute enough to recognize from my accent that I came from England. He sold the goods which he carried in

a small box under his arm as we journeyed along,
never releasing my arm. The cacophony of conversa-
tional noise which filled the air posed no problems to
him as he was able not only to identify numerous
languages, but also communicate in them with the
people he passed. Wheeling and dealing, he eventually brought me to the steps of the Dome of the Rock
where triumphantly he returned me to my leader-
less group. How he knew where to find Sari, where
he learned his languages, how he developed his sales
skills, from whom he gained his keen insights into
human nature, where he learned so much about
America and England are mysteries to me. But this
one thing I know, he was a very astute, knowledgeable, disciplined, sharp, attractive, young rascal who
reminded me once again that wisdom is more than
book learning and education is more than schooling.
In fact, one of my friends, a successful American busi-
nessman, said, "If I could take two or three kids like
him back home I could double my business in twelve
months." He was only partly joking.

It is unfortunate that western society, because of
its marvelous educational skills, has often fallen into
the trap of confusing knowledge with academic excellence, and regarding education and schooling as
synonymous. As we saw in the previous chapter,
however, Scripture teaches that there is a spiritual
base to true knowledge and, therefore, it is possible
for the "educated" to be singularly unwise and the
"uneducated" remarkably knowledgeable about life
in all its dimensions. This is because spiritual princi-

ples, when adequately grasped and adhered to, bring many other factors into operation. Solomon listed some of them in his opening words: "for attaining wisdom and discipline; for understanding words of insight; for acquiring a disciplined and prudent life, doing what is right and just and fair; for giving prudence to the simple, knowledge and discretion to the young, let the wise listen and add to their learning and let the discerning get guidance . . . " (Proverbs 1:2–5).

Derek Kidner, in his helpful book *Proverbs*, wrote that these opening verses should be seen as "breaking up the plain daylight of wisdom into its rainbow of constituent colors." As anyone who has looked through a prism or stared at a rainbow knows, light which is in itself colorless is composed of the brightest of colors: red, orange, yellow, green, blue, indigo, and violet. In the same way when Solomon spoke of wisdom, he showed that it included discipline, understanding, insight, prudence, and discretion.

It is interesting to note that Solomon, along with all his other pursuits, found time to learn about "plant life, from the cedar of Lebanon to the hyssop that grows out of walls. He also taught about animals and birds, reptiles and fish" (1 Kings 4:33). His natural curiosity and skilled powers of observation made him one of the world's experts on these matters. But when he spoke of wisdom, he was not thinking of the accumulation of facts and figures of such things as plants and reptiles. He had in mind the instruction that he had received from the Lord which required a disciplined response. This was not always pleasant as his famous advice to his son clearly showed: "My son, do not despise the Lord's discipline and do not resent his rebuke, because the Lord disciplines those he loves as a father the son he delights in" (Proverbs 3:11, 12).

Sometimes the instruction came loudly and clearly in the form of rebukes or correction and he recognized that the only way to adequately recognize the Lord and accordingly grow in wisdom was to take the rebuke and heed the correction.

In a day when it is more common for people to disregard the Word of God than to read it, and much more popular for people to "disagree with what the Bible says" than to accept its correction, it is frightening to realize that for all its sophistication, our generation may not be at all wise because it knows so little of the willing spirit that brings its life into obedience to the revealed will of God.

To rebuke is to be primarily negative. Many coaches feel it is necessary to tell their players not to do certain things with such well-chosen words as, "You dummy, sit on this bench until you learn not to do a stupid thing." This is an unmistakable rebuke which may or may not be deserved. But a good coach never rebukes without correcting. After a few minutes to allow the rebuke to sink in, he will go to his chastened player and add, "what you should have done was such and such a thing." After being rebuked and corrected the player is now more aware and if he disciplines himself to remember and put into practice what he now knows, he will be a wiser performer. Not only athletes should remember that "Whoever loves discipline loves knowledge, but he who hates correction is stupid" (Proverbs 12:1).

The famous story of Solomon's handling of the awkward predicament of the two women who came to him, both claiming the same child, is a marvelous illustration of another aspect of wisdom. When he first asked the Lord for wisdom, he stated his desire to be able to "discern between" which is basically the same expression as the one translated "insight." With consummate skill, he went quickly from the obvious premise that the child could not have two mothers to the conclusion that one of the women was at best mistaken, and at worst, for some ulterior motive, lying. He knew how to find out if one of them was lying by calling for a sword to cut the child in half and divide it equally between the two claimants. Quite naturally, the real mother reacted with horror at such a suggestion while the other kept silent. No doubt Solomon had no intention of dividing the child, and he knew that any right-thinking person would realize this, but he also knew that no mother could ever be accused of thinking clearly at such a time! Emotions, not rationality, govern the moment. The emotional woman, blurting out her dismay, clearly showed herself to be the real mother, while the other woman was still trying to figure out what Solomon was doing. He was able to "discern between" the women and display insight into their characters. The wisdom that comes from knowing the Lord is particularly necessary for discerning between that which is right or wrong, that which is good or bad, that which is true or false. Many people in our world don't worry about such things, as they much prefer to operate on such principles as "if it feels good, it must be all right" or "everybody's doing it so it must be fine." To know what the Lord says is good or evil and to be able to recognize the one or the other and to separate them when they come in confusing form and complex manner is the essence of the wisdom of which Solomon spoke.

There was a time in former generations when parents called their daughters by such names as Faith and Prudence, but in more recent times Debbie, Becky, Cindy, and Susie have become much more common. Perhaps Prudence went out of fashion about the same time that the word *prude* began to produce sniggers. Whatever the reason, it is particularly unfortunate that the word *prudence* has also fallen into disuse, because it is a fine word for a superb attribute.

When Isaiah wrote prophetically of the Suffering Servant, he predicted, "See, my servant will act wisely (prudently); he will be raised and lifted up and highly exalted" (Isaiah 52:13). The Servant's wisdom or prudence was going to lead him to a place of exaltation or success. The same thought is found in Genesis where Eve, looking at the tree, noted that it "was good for food and pleasing to the eye and, also, desirable for gaining wisdom" (Genesis 3:6). Eve, having been seduced by the serpent into a position where she felt that Jehovah had been limiting her development and stunting her growth as a person, had embarked on a search that would lead her to insight and wisdom. This, she believed, would make her a success rather than a person damned to meaninglessness and frustration by adherence to the Lord's principles. Eve sought success and missed it. The servant, for all intents and purposes, failed and yet was a resounding success. This leads to the famous question "What is success?" To Eve it was self-determination through independent attitudes and bold pursuit of her own goals. Success and wisdom in her eyes came from a dismissal of God as God and the establishing of her own reign in her own life to do her own thing her own way. She was going to be her own person, carving her own destiny, making her own rules and judging her own actions. Like a ballplayer making his own rules and keeping his own score, calling his own shots and deciding every close call, it would appear that she could not fail to succeed. Yet fail she did.

On the other hand, the Suffering Servant hanging bruised and defeated, despised and rejected on a cross, the ultimate of shame and the epitome of failure was actually exhibiting success par excellence. From the depths of his soul came the triumphant cry "Finished," a bold statement that he completed the work the Father had given him to do. Not for him the path of self-determination; only the desire to do the Father's will. Confronted with his tree, he, unlike Eve at her tree, chose not his own way but humbly and courageously decided, "Not My will but Thine be done." In spiritual terms, the wisdom that spells prudence or success is the wisdom that discovers and does the divine will. Success is not the achieving of personal goals unrelated to the purposes of God, but rather the subjugating of personal objectives to the mind of the Lord. Solomon spelled it out as "doing what is right and just and fair!"

This morning as I was eating breakfast in a motel in Knoxville, Tennessee, I was invited to join two men at an adjacent table. They had attended some of the meetings I was addressing in the city and wanted to talk with me about the application of the messages. During the course of the conversation one of the men, a former college football coach, told me of an incident in a high school basketball game where he noticed that the clock was not being started and stopped correctly. As the score was very close and the time was almost expired, every second counted. Watching both the game and the clock, he realized that the man in charge was saving a few seconds each time the clock came into play and on challenging him found himself summarily expelled from the arena under the tender care of two burly policemen. It is a sad commentary on sport at the high school level when success (which is spelled "WINNING") becomes the altar upon which such things as "right, justice and fair play" are sacrificed. Yet, what can we expect from a society that has determined its own standards of success in every field of endeavor and rejected the eternal principles established by the Lord?

Years ago when I was a young Royal Marine, I saw a fascinating illustration of the old saying, "Discretion is the better part of valor." We were being instructed in the deadly art of throwing hand grenades. Standing in a specially designed pit surrounded by sandbags, we were shown how to stand, feet apart, holding the grenade in the right hand with the thumb and forefinger of the left circling the pin. When ready, we jumped in the air, found our target in a split second, drew out the pin and hurled the lethal bomb. There was a loud thump as the bomb exploded and the whistle of the base plug as it screeched overhead, then the remarks of the instructor which occasionally outdid both thump and screech. One nervous recruit did everything right except he threw the grenade straight up in the air and when it landed on the parapet of the dugout, he, turning to seek the instructor's approval, found himself alone. The instructor had dived for cover, showing much more discretion than valor. Solomon explained it this way: "A prudent man sees danger and takes refuge, but the simple keep going and suffer for it" (Proverbs 22:3).

The ability to take the appropriate action in any given set of circumstances is another way of describing "discretion." This requires the ability to "size up" the situation, knowledge of the options available and, also, the capacity to choose correctly and act accordingly. Many an erudite man has failed to exhibit this aspect of spiritual knowledge and insight and has left his life in ruins. Many an attractive woman has been praised for her beauty and sought out by her admirers, but because she could not see the potential dangers of the designs of her admirers, she proved the truth of the proverb: "Like a gold ring in a pig's snout is a beautiful woman who shows no discretion" (Proverbs 11:22).

The knowledge that comes through the fear of the Lord and the knowledge of the Holy One is a many-splendored thing. As we look at it closely and see its many-faceted beauty, there is a real possibility that we may become discouraged and decide it is well beyond our capabilities and that we should just settle for doing the best we can. But to think like this is to ignore one of the most beautiful aspects of this wisdom, namely that it is available to all who will be earnest about their desire to acquire it. The wisdom that comes from the Lord is not reserved for an intellectual elite or confined to a select company of the initiated, but is readily given to those who will respond to the invitation to learn God's way: "Wisdom has built her house; she has hewn out its seven pillars. She has prepared her meat and mixed her wine; she has also set her table. She has sent out her maids, and she calls from the highest point of the city. 'Let all who are simple come in here!' she says to those who lack judgment" (Proverbs 9:1–4).

These sentiments were to be repeated in later years by the Lord Jesus when he said: "Come to me, all you who are weary and burdened, and I will give you rest. Take my yoke upon you and learn of me and you will find rest for your souls" (Matthew 11:28, 29). To all who seek truth and will humble themselves at the feet of the One who calls to humble repentance and wholehearted commitment, there is a promise of true wisdom and real knowledge; an offer that people ought not to be able to refuse!

THREE

Life Forces

Listen, my son, to your father's instruction, and do not forsake your mother's teaching.

Proverbs 1:8

Philosophers talk about "life force" or *élan vital* in tones so hushed that most people don't know they are talking or that *élan vital* exists. Recently, however, those same people have been flocking to the movies to see the fabulously successful *Star Wars*, a brilliant piece of cinematic fantasy projecting, in a strangely compelling manner, the struggle between the "Force" and assorted forces of evil. More and more people are coming to believe in some kind of forces that control or influence their lives, whether they be philosophical, astrological, magical, spiritual, or mystical. The forces are usually ill-defined because they have been ill-conceived, but this does not deter the believers from being convinced of the reality of their experiences.

The Proverbs are clear where much modern thinking is vague. They state, powerfully, that it is

God who is behind all things. "Many are the plans in a man's heart, but it is the LORD's purpose that prevails" (Proverbs 19:21). Rather than allowing a broad generalization of unspecified forces as the object of faith, they insist on a relationship with Jehovah called "the knowledge of the Holy One." This "Holy One" is not a deity produced through human ingenuity to meet his deepest emotional needs, but rather the Self-Existent who revealed himself to the patriarchs as the One through whom blessings would come to all nations. Through his intervention in human affairs and the glad response of mankind to his intervention, people would come to know him in the person of his Son, the Christ, the Savior of the world. And make no mistake about it, his purposes wrapped up in his Son will prevail. It is this powerful and unequivocal message that is the hallmark of the Scriptures and the marked contrast to the conventional wisdom.

The outworking of his purposes for mankind in general, and individuals in particular, takes place, of course, in a world where many forces operate under the direction of the Lord. The tumultuous crosscurrents of these often conflicting forces is the environment in which the wise person lives successfully and the unwise person so sadly flounders. This is why I often think that navigating through life is like sailing a boat. I am by no stretch of the imagination a sailor, but on my annual summer vacation I enjoy the relaxation of taking out a small Sunfish on the water of Wrightsville Beach in North Carolina. The change of pace from the busy pastorate to the tranquil motion of the boat, the exchange of the lapping of water on the hull for the shrill insistence of the ever-present phone is one of the most relaxing experiences I can imagine. But I have learned not to be too relaxed. Tides have a habit of changing imperceptibly, sea breezes are notoriously capricious, currents lurk in pleasant waters and hidden sandbanks await the overrelaxed sailor! It is necessary to read the wind and set the sail to maximize its flow. The movements of the tides must be carefully checked so that the rudder can be held in the right position and a keen eye should be kept on the water all the time in case the bottom suddenly appears. Failure to allow for the force of tide, current, wind, and breeze spells disaster, but correct knowledge of the situation produces smooth sailing.

Some of the most powerful of life forces are the formative influences to which everybody is exposed in their early years. Psychologists are of the opinion that most of a person's characteristics are determined at a very tender age. It follows, therefore, that parental influence is of the utmost importance not only in the tender years of infancy, but also the tumultuous days of youth and adolescence. That Solomon clearly understood this is demonstrated by the numerous appeals he made in Proverbs as a father to his son and his powerful instruction, "Listen my son to your father's instruction, and do not forsake your mother's teaching" (Proverbs 1:8). The fact that he used both father and mother in this proverb should not be attributed solely to his poetic use of parallelism—a device loved by the Hebrews and cleverly used in the Proverbs. It should be seen as a reminder that the ideal influence comes from a "father's instruction" and a "mother's teaching." For there to be balanced parental training there needs to be a healthy environment in which both parents bring their gifts, their skills, their spiritual insights, and natural abilities to bear on the life of the child.

I know many single parents who struggle to bring about the proper parental influence so that their children may derive the right training in their impressionable years, and many do a commendable job in difficult circumstances, but they are always prepared to admit that they cannot be both mother and father, however devoted they are to their children and however completely they give themselves to the task. There is a similar problem in families where absentee fathers put in occasional visits to their families so that to all intents and purposes they are strangers to their children. The young people in such situations must be deficient in their upbringing and steps should be taken wherever possible to ensure that the forces of correct parental influence are available when needed most.

Solomon wrote that this correct parental influence incorporated "instruction" and "teaching." It is worth noting that even in a day when there is an increased tendency to pay the teacher to educate, the psychologist to counsel, the coach to discipline, and the pastor to catechise, the major responsibility to teach and instruct still remains with the parents.

Those parents who surrender the control of formative influences to people outside the family circle, without adequate control and supervision of the influence being exerted in their children, ask for trouble and, if this is the case, they find it in later years.

I am not suggesting that only parents should do the teaching, for I believe that the term "father," while it refers primarily to the natural father, can also be applied legitimately to spiritual fathers, too. Paul the Apostle took a particular interest in the development and well-being of Timothy, a young man of nervous disposition and indifferent health. He called him, "My true son in the faith" (1 Timothy 1:2) and it is obvious from such statements as, "You, however, know all about my teaching, my way of life, my purpose, faith, patience, love and endurance" (2 Timothy 3:10) that he had made a considerable investment of time and energy in his spiritual son.

We should not overlook the formative influences of such historical figures as Founding Fathers and Church Fathers as we remember that, although their influence is to most people either totally hidden or relatively obscure, their contribution to life, as it now is, was by no means insignificant. Perhaps the greatest incentive and encouragement to those of us who endeavor to be the right kind of godly, righteous, balanced parental influences on our children, is to be found in the promise, "Train up a child in the way he should go and when he is old he will not turn from it" (Proverbs 22:6). This should be balanced with the stark warning, "The rod of correction imparts wis-

dom, but a child left to itself disgraces his mother"
(Proverbs 29:15).

My first attempt at sailing was almost my last attempt at anything. It was during my Marine training
in South Devon, a particularly beautiful part of England. We had been training very hard all week and
when the opportunity to take out a Royal Navy
whaler was presented, about a dozen of us jumped
aboard and headed for the open water. As the breeze
was blowing briskly offshore, we soon filled our sails
and headed out to sea at a spanking pace. After some
time, one of the more observant members of the
crew pointed out that we could no longer see the
land and another suggested it might be a good idea
if we headed back towards England! He was dis-
missed as a "chicken" and we continued our voyage.
Eventually, somebody asked, "How do you turn this
thing around?" "Put it about" he was promptly corrected. "I don't care what you call it, just somebody
do it," he replied. It was then that we discovered
nobody knew how to turn it around or put it about!
We tried and disaster resulted because we went
about it the wrong way, narrowly missed capsizing,
broke a mainstay and were within inches of losing
one of our men overboard as the boom swung across
and hit him in the pit of his stomach. With the mainstay broken, the wind suddenly dropped and like the
Ancient Mariner we were becalmed. A doleful bell
buoy tolled its mournful warning, but instead of getting louder, it became fainter; and as darkness fell we
realized the tides had turned and the current was

taking us into the shipping lanes. After a cold, cold night we were rescued and towed back into port, much to the delight of the hundreds of holiday-makers who lined the pier.

Youth, foolhardiness, sheer ignorance, misguided macho, and rank immaturity had combined to take us to the edge of tragedy. We had no knowledge of the prevailing winds, we knew nothing about the currents, we had not checked on the tides, and nobody had bothered to learn how to sail the boat, so we were nothing more than helpless victims of forces beyond our control.

In addition to the potentially blessed influence of the right kind of father and mother, there are also the malevolent influences that operate in life like hidden currents and to these influences Solomon turned his attention: "My son, if sinners entice you, do not give in to them . . . do not go along with them, do not set foot on their paths" (Proverbs 1:10–15). Evil enticements are often extremely attractive and the unwary or the uninitiated are often swept away by them before they know what is happening. With great skill Solomon sketched a picture of the enticing appeal of "friends" who say, "Come with us" and in the invitation offer that kind of acceptance which everybody craves. To the enticing thought of acceptance were added the promise of excitement, "Let's waylay some harmless soul," and the offer of personal gain, "We will get all sorts of valuable things and fill our houses with plunder." The picture may be overdrawn for our western sensibilities, but toned down ever so slightly would sound very similar to the sort of offers that many businessmen receive in the normal course of their activities. The promise of popularity and the pleasing prospect of "having some fun" and "making a buck or two" have been too much for many a teenager, finding out for the first time that peer pressure is very closely related to fear pressure. The fear of being left out of the mainstream and missing out on the action has led the unsuspecting into difficulties, and then the fear of being rejected has made them afraid to get out of the situation. It is difficult to warn people who think that you are spoiling their fun, and almost impossible to stop people from doing what they have already decided they are going to do, even though they may be partially aware of the consequences. With touching frustration, Solomon wrote, "How useless to spread a net in full view of all the birds" (Proverbs 1:17), inferring, of course, that birds have the sense not to get into trouble, which is more than can be said for those who are susceptible to evil enticements.

There is only one way to counter these evil life forces and it is spelled out bluntly in the proverb, "Don't give in to them." Temptations are not easily rejected and everybody at sometime in his experience has been aware of the enticements but has succumbed even against his better judgment. I am convinced that the reason for this is not hard to find when we remember that we are not only charged with resisting the forces of evil but also responding to the Lord. The two factors are related, because it is only as we yield in obedience to the Lord that we discover the strength he imparts to the obedient. But if we are not reckoning with him and we are disregarding his instruction, we will inevitably yield to the evil forces. It comes down, therefore, to a matter of priorities and decision. We can make desires and aspirations our priorities and then with nothing constant to guide, we drift out among the powerful currents. Alternatively, we can set our sails to catch every whisper of the Lord and every gust of the powerful wind of his Spirit. God has promised that the wind of the Spirit will always be greater than the drift of the current, so we must face the reality of the situation and admit that if we are yielding to temptation it is due to our resisting God's way in our lives.

I realize that this is very blunt talk, but it is impossible to read the Proverbs without confronting blunt truth. "How long will you simple ones love your simple ways? How long will mockers delight in mockery and fools hate knowledge?" (Proverbs 1:22). This is very straightforward and poses no problems of interpretation to anyone who can read in a straight line!

These blunt words come from the lips of Wisdom who, for the sake of striking communication, is personified as calling "aloud in the street" and raising "her voice in the public squares." These words, when understood, remind us of the ongoing proclamation of God's truth which is available to people in their daily lives, in the streets, the public squares, and the gateways of the cities. This proclamation is found in the Word of God which is so readily available in our western world. Anyone can go into any public library and read the Word if they don't wish to go into a bookstore and purchase their own copy. On street corners there are hundreds of churches with open doors and open Bibles placed in strategic positions, so that whoever enters can see and read the proclamation of God's Wisdom. Although the Bible continues to be the biggest seller, for many people it does not have the influence it is designed to have, because while it is bought and revered, so often it is not read and believed.

Some people are reluctant to read the Word of God because of its straightforwardness. They are insulted by its descriptions of them and unwilling to accept its promises and predictions, and I must say this is perfectly understandable. Who wants to be told such things as, "Since they hated knowledge and did not choose to fear the LORD, since they would not accept my advice and spurned my rebuke, they will eat the fruit of their ways and be filled with the fruit of their schemes" (Proverbs 1:29–31). Certainly not the ones who choose not to fear the Lord! Yet on the other hand, those who respond to the Word of God in trust and obedience testify to the truth of the words, "If you had responded to my rebuke I would have poured out my heart to you and made my thoughts known to you" (Proverbs 1:23). They have experienced the unspeakable joy of sensing the heartthrob of the Lord himself and have discovered that they have begun to grasp his thoughts and follow his ways.

The fact of the matter is that when we start to think about life forces there is no greater than the living power of the Word of God. To those who reject it the powerful predictions come true, and to those who respond the winsome discovery of the reality of God's presence and power become part of life on a daily basis. I know of no more fitting words to sum up these thoughts than, "For the waywardness of the simple will kill them, and the complacency of fools will destroy them; but whosoever listens to me will live in safety and be at ease, without fear of harm" (Proverbs 1:32, 33).

FOUR

Decisions, Decisions

*For the waywardness of the simple will
kill them, and the complacency of fools
will destroy them; but whosoever listens to
me will live in safety and be at ease, without fear of harm.*

Proverbs 1:32, 33

Recently a pastor-friend of mine was so desperately ill and his life was draining away so rapidly that
if nothing was done he would die within a matter of
hours. The surgeon in charge, however, knew that
the patient was terribly weak and it was doubtful if
he was strong enough to survive the surgical proce-
dures required. A split-second decision was necessary.

The runner was approaching third base as the
right fielder made the catch to dismiss the second
man in the bottom of the ninth inning. One run sepa-
rated the teams. If the third base coach waved the
runner on to home plate and he made it, the game
would be tied up, but if he came short the season was
over. A split-second decision was needed.

Surgeons and third base coaches live in a world of quick decisions, although the decisions they make are not the products of impulse. In the surgeon's case, years of training and years of experience together with all manner of data combine to enable him to quickly calculate the mathematical odds of survival in all the alternatives open to him, and on this basis he acts. The coach has locked up in the computer of his baseball brain information concerning the speed of the runner, the skill of the catcher, the strength of the fielder's arm, the distance from the corner, and the length of the winter if he makes the wrong decision! On the basis of this information he decides.

Most people rarely have to make split-second, life or death, win or lose decisions, but they are constantly required to decide on matters of varying importance. Big decisions like whether to marry the homecoming queen, whether to accept the promotion and the move to New York, or whether to sell the family car or give it a tune-up and gamble it will survive the winter. Small ones like whether to eat dessert, use a six or seven iron, or wear a purple or red tie with their pink shirt and green suit.

Life is so full of decisions of varying magnitude that many people feel inadequate to cope with them and some of them simply trip out into a never-never land of irresponsibility. Others are so conscious of their need for help that they attend seminars on decision making or read the latest books that promise all kinds of help, while still others spend small fortunes in analysts' offices employing the counselor to make the decisions for them. In this kind of situation it is particularly encouraging to note that the Scriptures have something to say on the subject. Not, of course, on base runners or beauty queens, but decisions relating to the moral dilemmas and the spiritual realities with which everybody is continually confronted. Solomon talked about the different paths that people take and dramatically showed that the decisions we make have such far-reaching consequences, they can mean the difference between following "the paths of life" or finishing up on "the paths to the spirits of the dead" (Proverbs 2:18, 19).

When we have to decide about simple, practical matters such as cars and ties, the decision is relatively straightforward because the alternatives are reasonably clear. But decisions relating to the paths of life are often more difficult due, in part, to the reluctance which some people express towards accepting that there are clear-cut moral and spiritual options. Living as we do in a society that is wallowing in a sea of relativity, there has been a turning away from the concept of absolute standards and the specific absolute statements of Scripture.

Such powerful concepts as good and evil, right and wrong, heaven and hell have become as blurred as a badly focused movie, and the result has been confusing and discouraging to many people. Good is determined by how it strikes the participant at any given moment, so "if it feels good it must be good for you." If it isn't feeling so good then it isn't so good, although it is unlikely that it will be regarded as anything as unpleasant as the opposite of good and called evil. Ironically, those who most vociferously deny absolute values like good and evil speak out forcibly against such people and things as Hitler, Idi Amin, apartheid, and nuclear energy in terms sounding suspiciously absolute for lips so relatively trained.

Spiritual truth has also suffered mainly because its most popular aspects, love and tolerance, have become so distorted that everybody is being encouraged to lovingly allow and encourage everybody else to believe whatever they choose to believe. The resultant confusion has produced situations where people are free to believe that either God does exist or God does not exist; with the idea that it doesn't matter whether he does or he doesn't because his existence is more or less irrelevant.

To insist on the basis of the law of noncontradiction, that we can't have it both ways, is to risk the charge of being biased, prejudiced or other nasty things; and to suggest that because something is right the opposite must be wrong and to apply it to people and ideas is to be regarded as boorish and philistine. Paradoxically, however, those who hold to ill-determined and broad-minded views usually have little compunction in castigating their more biblically oriented neighbors without feeling that they are being prejudiced or boorish. While good and evil, right and wrong go through the wringer and come out as something flattened beyond recognition or definition, heaven and hell have become respectively "whatever you want it to be" or a "relic of medieval, monastic masochism."

On the basis of such blurred information it is practically impossible to see how people can make decisions of lasting importance and feel a sense of confidence that they have done the right thing and will accomplish something good. If Scripture is used as the basis, however, the story is totally different. Right and wrong, good and evil, heaven and hell are spoken of with authority and assurance and they are also clearly related to a person's experience of the Lord. To "fear" and to "know" him is to be led in the right path and to fail to be rightly related to him is to be led in the opposite direction. Assuming this to be true, the potential path-walker, desirous to know how he may discover the Lord, may know his truth and may walk gladly therein.

There are two possible approaches to the discovery of God. The first one, which appears to be the most obvious, is that man should use his considerable ingenuity and skill to search God out. The other, but more valid approach, is to recognize that man cannot, through human effort and rational skill, ever fathom the mystery of God and, therefore, the onus rests upon God to reveal himself. There is something about this second approach which thinking people find hard to accept. Perhaps they feel that they are committing intellectual suicide if they open themselves to the possibility of divine revelation rather than depending exclusively on human rationalization. But it should be made clear that when we accept the premise that God can only be known through his self-revelation, it does not mean that man is freed from the responsibility of using his God-given powers of thought, imagination, research, and study. On the contrary, he has to learn to approach the areas of God's revelation with reverent, careful skill and commitment in order that he might grasp with his whole being more and more of the things that God wishes him to know. It should never be forgotten, therefore, that "The LORD gives wisdom, and from his mouth come knowledge and understanding" (Proverbs 2:6). The nature of God's self-revelation has been the subject of debate over the centuries, but there are certain areas of human experience in which we can certainly be enriched through careful study of what God has revealed.

The first area of revelation is creation. Nobody who has eyes to see or ears to hear can have missed grasping something of the majesty and power of God, clearly demonstrated in the things he has made. Granted, the knowledge of God which is limited to creation is inadequate, for it could leave us with a belief in a power of grandeur and beauty both terrifying in its might and overwhelming in its magnitude, but little else. There is, however, a further revelation of God in human conscience. This inherent sense of such things as fairness and unfairness, rights and justice, moral integrity and ethical standard are, according to Scripture, built into our humanity as an evidence of the nature of God's being. From creation and conscience we have the knowledge that God is a majestic power, greater and grander than his handiwork with a built-in sense of morality and integrity. The unfolding of the Scripture goes further and shows that God, far from being only a moral force, is the One who loves to make covenants or promises to his people. From the earliest part of the Old Testament there is a consistent emphasis on the Lord's insistence on making covenants with such people as Adam, Noah, Abraham, Moses, and David. Each of these covenants shows that God is intimately concerned with the affairs of mankind and has every intention of working in and through man to bring his eternal purposes to consummation. To the Old Testament covenants must be added the New Covenant God made through Christ. The pinnacle of the divine revelation is in Christ.

In the stupendous act of God assuming our humanity in Jesus of Nazareth, with all its limitations and frustrations, he showed us aspects of his being which man could never have discovered any other way. The glory of God veiled in human flesh became tolerable to frail humanity and the demonstration of deity in the form of humanity became understandable to mankind. In Christ, the great Creator showed himself to be, in addition to a great moral force, intimately concerned with the affairs of his creation, the lover of men's souls and procurer of their salvation. In Christ, man has the chance to see the glory of God and survive the experience. Even veiled as it was in the Incarnate Lord, there were times when the intensity of God's righteousness and holiness was such that men fell before him, beseeching him to depart from them because of the great sense of sinfulness that engulfed them when they were in his presence. Even the demons knew who he was and begged him to leave them alone. Any attempt by man to find the right path should, therefore, be rooted in the revelation that God has given of himself in all these areas. As he reverently and carefully gives himself to the study of God's truth as seen in these aspects of his experience and devotes himself to the account of these things recorded in Scripture, so man can get on the right track and be equipped to make the right decisions.

Man's responsibility in these matters is carefully outlined in Proverbs 2:1–5: "My son, if you accept my words and store up my commands within you, turning your ear to wisdom and applying your heart to understanding; and if you call out for insight and cry aloud for understanding, and if you look for it as for silver and search for it as for hidden treasure, then you will understand the fear of the LORD and find the knowledge of God." Without going into any detailed explanation of this passage of Scripture, I would like to point out the fundamental requirements and conditions which, when fulfilled, lead to the discovery of the right way to go: "Accept my words" . . . arrive at an intelligent conclusion concerning the truth. "Store up my commands" . . . build this truth into the decision-making process. "Turning your ear" . . . choosing to give attention to God's Word. "Applying your heart" . . . taking the truth to its moral and spiritual conclusion. "Call out for insight" . . . show intensity of desire for the truth. "Cry aloud for understanding" . . . let your desires and intentions be known. "Look for it as silver" . . . show a marked degree of enthusiasm and determination. "Search . . . as for hidden treasure". . . be prepared to work at it.

At first sight these conditions appear overwhelming, and it is precisely because of this that many people give up the search for God's gift of wisdom through the knowledge of him before they have even started. But I have been particularly impressed with the fact that where there are those who have a genuine desire to know the Lord and serve him, there appears to be a sharpening of the intellectual capabilities, a nerving of the faint heart, and an instilling of determination where previously there had been only halfheartedness.

Alex Rodgers, a friend of mine from Scotland, is a marvelous example of this phenomenon. As a young man recently graduated from high school with no great ambition, he got a job in the laboratory of a nearby factory and proceeded to work in a manner that was satisfactory, but little more. Through the influence of some friends he was converted to Christ and recognized quickly that if he was going to be a Christian he would need to be a serious disciple of the Risen Lord. He joined a church and began to apply himself to his newfound faith. As time went on he became aware of a sense of calling to the ministry, but on sharing these convictions with his pastor he was dismayed to discover that his denomination required candidates for the ministry to have a B.A. in some area of general study and a B.D. in theological study. He had no desire whatsoever to embark on a university career, but did so because he recognized that if he wanted to be a pastor, it was the way he would have to go. Never having studied philosophy he was appalled to discover that he was required to take courses in this subject, but to everybody's surprise, not least his own, he demonstrated such commitment and native ability that he sailed through his philosophy degree and did so well that he was offered a scholarship to Oxford to pursue doctoral studies in philosophy. He had no interest in this opportunity because, as he kept telling people, "All I want to do is preach the Gospel," so he declined the invitation, did his theological work and embarked on a pastorate. Shortly afterwards he accepted a post teaching religious education to teachers training to teach religious education.

As the experience of Alex Rodgers and countless other people has confirmed, "Where there's a will, there's a way," and to the surprise of the willing, the way is greater than their intentions and far beyond their known capabilities. Jesus summarized it in typically succinct fashion when he said, "Blessed are those who hunger and thirst for righteousness, for they will be filled" (Matthew 5:6).

There is a marked difference between the sipping and snacking that characterizes much spiritual searching today and the hungering and thirsting of which the Master spoke. This may be due to the fact that the society in which we live is so given to the veneration of immediacy and the demand for instantaneous experience, that there is a marked lack of enthusiasm for anything that savors of spiritual work and smacks of patience and forbearance. If spiritual experience can be expedited to produce quick growth and speedy maturity, it tends to be popular. True, we all know that "Rome wasn't built in a day," but when it comes to building lives of character and depth through the principles God has ordained, we see too much impatience and too little forbearance, too much growth that resembles the easy sprouting of the weed rather than the steady development of the oak.

God's insistence that we demonstrate serious application of mind and will to the discovery of his truth should not be interpreted as his way of making us struggle so that we'll appreciate it all the more when we find it. The immensity of all that God has to show of himself and his purposes is so beyond human grasp that only the ones who will stick with it will begin to understand, and the practical implications of discovering God's way for our lives are so great that without commitment to him and his way there is no possibility of their being followed. This does not mean that spiritual growth and experience is reserved for an intellectual elite or a secret society of the initiated. God does not expect from his people academic excellence above their capabilities, nor does he demand acts of devotion and sacrifice that will merit the gift of wisdom and knowledge through him. But he does insist that those who go his way mean business because he means business.

Plato limited access to his academy to those who were "geometricians," and many other schools of learning have understandably developed demanding standards before would-be students can enroll, but in the matter of knowing God there are no barriers other than man's unwillingness, and no restrictions other than those imposed by man on himself. The availability of the wisdom from above to all people is wonderfully stated in the Proverb, "To you, O men, I call out; I raise my voice to all mankind. You who are simple, gain prudence; You who are foolish, gain understanding" (Proverbs 8:4, 5).

It is unfortunate that some people become discouraged when they discover that spiritual experience is not as attractively packaged as meat in a supermarket. Suffering under the mistaken impression that they are free to wander among the shelves where God's blessings are stored in exciting variety and fill their carts full of good things which God, who sits at the checkout counter, won't even charge them for, they feel they have the inalienable right to be helped by God on their own terms and become resentful of anyone who says differently and even become upset with God if he doesn't deliver us when they think he should. But we should never be deterred by the fact that the experience of God has to be dug out like silver and searched for as assiduously as hidden treasure, because the promise of what God has available for his people is superb. To those who go God's way, the Word of God says, "Then you will understand what is right and just and fair—every good path. For wisdom will enter your heart, and knowledge will be pleasant to your soul. Discretion will protect you, and understanding will guard you" (Proverbs 2:9–11).

To those who may still be reticent about making life-changing decisions based on what God has to say, let me say that the outworking of all these things is directly related to your commitment to the Lord and his resultant involvement in your lives. For it is "He [who] holds victory in store for the upright, he is a shield to those whose walk is blameless, for he guards the course of the just and protects the way of his faithful ones" (Proverbs 2:7, 8).

Some years ago my friend Glenn Wilcox, who owns and operates "Wilcox World Tours," asked me if I would like to lead a group of people to the Middle East on a seminar based on the journeys of Paul. I liked the idea very much, but I was reluctant to undertake the responsibility for the tour as I had done that kind of thing before and I didn't have time to do it again. Glenn, sensing my hesitation, tried to impress upon me that my only responsibility would be to oversee the teaching and his office would handle everything else. I still wasn't persuaded until he said, "Stuart, you don't seem to understand. My wife and I will be on board with you. We will look after all the arrangements ourselves." That was good enough for me, so I led the tour, and Glenn and Pauline were as good as their word.

The promises of God are bound up in his presence in the life of the believer through the Holy Spirit. The Lord Jesus, immediately before concluding his earthly ministry, told his disciples, "Surely I will be with you always, to the very end of the age" (Matthew 28:20). With this kind of assurance that the One who reveals and dispenses truth is committed to it in our lives and continues to reside in our lives to empower us to obey, it should not be too hard to make the biggest decision of them all, "I have decided to follow Jesus, no turning back, no turning back."

FIVE

Healthy, Wealthy, and Wise

A good name is more desirable than great riches; to be esteemed is better than silver or gold. Rich and poor have this in common: The LORD *is the Maker of them all.*

Proverbs 22:1, 2

One of the best-known proverbs must be "Early to bed, early to rise, Makes a man healthy, wealthy, and wise." The promises of health, wealth, and wisdom to those who join the ranks of the early retirers and risers must be particularly appealing to many people in our contemporary society. There is no doubt that one of the greatest concerns of modern man is his health. It is estimated that in the United States $200 billion are spent on health care each year. The medical field has grown into such big business that it employs 4.8 million people; and it appears that in many places, more staff is needed to meet the demands of the people who are concerned about their physical well-being.

Much more interest has been shown in preventive medicine in recent years. This is probably due in part to the increasing costs of medical treatment, but the writings of such people as Dr. Kenneth Cooper have also been greatly instrumental. In his book *Aerobics,* Dr. Cooper communicated his message of the benefits of exercise so effectively many other authors have followed in his trail, and literally millions of readers have donned their Adidas and taken to the highways and byways of America. A recent survey showed that over 17 million people are jogging. Many of these are so serious they have trained themselve to run the 26 miles and 385 yards of the grueling marathons that are sponsored all over the country. The last time I was in Honolulu, I was amazed to see hundreds of people, young and old, running for their lives, and I discovered many of them have run in the Hawaiian Marathon.

Exercise has also become a major part of conversation. At a dinner party recently, the president of a bank asked me confidentially, "You look like a runner; how far do you run each day?" A few days later when I appeared on a national television show, the host suddenly asked me if I was a regular runner. On both occasions the conversation turned to the subject of exercise and I found, as I have found whenever I have traveled recently, that this is a subject on many people's minds. Of course, there are still many people who are less than enthusiastic about exercise. They appreciate the philosophy of Robert M. Hutchins who said, "Whenever the thought of exercise occurs to me, I lie down till it passes."

If health is a major concern of the average American, wealth is equally important. America is the "land of opportunity." The standard cliché that the United States is the country where "anyone can become President" is almost true, but there is no doubt it is the home of innumerable people who have become phenomenally successful in materialistic terms. The freedom of opportunity which enables a person with drive, skill, and determination to rise to spectacular heights is a fiercely defended freedom, whereas those members of the society who feel skeptical of this freedom pour scorn on its doctrines and heap insults on its proponents, with equal ferocity.

Since the days of the oil embargo and worldwide inflation, there have been increasing demands that something be done about rising costs and diminishing purchasing power; but more people are coming to the conclusion that the government cannot or will not do anything to solve the problem. People at the lower end of the financial scale are frankly worried about making ends meet, and those who are more affluent see their hard-earned dollars going the way of the Reichsmark and are busily stashing their savings in Geneva or buying Krugerrands. When a book written by Howard Ruff with the unlikely title *How to Prosper During the Coming Bad Years* becomes a best-seller, it doesn't take a degree in psychology or sociology to recognize that people want to prosper and are afraid that circumstances are such that they may find it increasingly difficult. The book is reinforced by a twice monthly newsletter called *The Ruff Times* and a television program called "Ruff House," in which financial advice is dispensed to those who are either wealthy and want to stay that way, or never have been wealthy and have no intention of staying *that* way!

If the best-selling lists give some indication of the prevailing interests of a society, then we must recognize that health concerns, as demonstrated by the success of *Aerobics* and innumerable diet books, and wealth concerns, as exhibited by Ruff's book and others like *Sylvia Porter's Money Book,* are at the front of people's thinking. To these concerns we must also add the search for answers or practical wisdom. Bookshelves are loaded with literature entitled, "Everything You Want to Know About . . . " and a proliferation of books in the self-improvement division whose titles usually begin with the words, "How to. . . . " The variety of "How to" books is bewildering, and it would seem that, assuming the writers know the right answers, there are no questions that need remain unanswered and no problems that need stay unsolved! Of course, there is always the old proverb that promises the three things that people seem to desire most—health, wealth, and wisdom—are readily available through better sleeping habits, but nobody believes that any more than they believe the popular books and seminars have all the answers.

The third chapter of Proverbs has been speaking about these things for many a long century, but unfortunately many people don't seem to know. When it comes to health, the instructions are perfectly clear, "Do not be wise in your own eyes; fear the

LORD and shun evil. This will bring health to your body and nourishment to your bones" (Proverbs 3:7, 8). The advice concerning wealth is equally straightforward: "Honor the LORD with your wealth, with the first fruits of all your crops; then your barns will be filled to overflowing and your vats will brim over with new wine" (Proverbs 3:9, 10). As we have seen, the book of Proverbs has a recurring theme relating to the meaning and discovery of wisdom, but there is no more beautiful or appealing description of wisdom's blessing than, "She is more precious than rubies; nothing you desire can compare with her. Long life is in her right hand; in her left hand are riches and honor. Her ways are pleasant ways, and all her paths are peace" (Proverbs 3:15–17). Far from promising health, wealth, and wisdom to those who sleep better, Proverbs reminds us that these things are the product of better spiritual insight and commitment, which will, among other things, have a lot to say about our sleeping habits.

Physical health is not one of the major emphases of Scripture, but it has, nevertheless, trenchant things to say on the subject. It is important that we should recognize the biblical view of man insists man is a whole person made up of "spirit, soul, and body," and careful study of Scripture shows that it is the interplay of these facets of our beings that makes us the people we are. It is difficult to imagine a person without a body or to visualize a body as being a person. The true person is not a physical entity driven solely by chemical reactions and electrical charges;

neither is he a spirit unwillingly enslaved in a body. A person is spirit, soul, and body and the degree in which all three interact determines the effectiveness of that person.

Modern science has shown that the physical body can exhibit symptoms that are not caused by physical consideration, but are rather the product of psychological distress. The word psychosomatic, which is becoming increasingly common in modern vocabulary, is in itself a joining together of the Greek words for soul and body. Perhaps the fact that Paul wrote that "your body is a temple of the Holy Spirit" (1 Corinthians 6:19) should have been taken more seriously by the medical profession years ago, for it clearly states that there is an interplay, not only of man's spirit, soul, and body, but also that the Holy Spirit is involved in the innermost recesses of man's being. When we understand the holistic aspect of man's being, we have little difficulty understanding what Solomon meant when he said that spiritual consideration, when properly adhered to, would have an effect on health and longevity.

There are many differing motivations that lead people to seek physical fitness. Some, like professional athletes, do it for the money; others, having heard that there is a special "high" associated with various athletic pursuits, do it for existential reasons; whereas others do it because they make a life-style out of following the latest fads. Solomon, however, relates physical well-being to the all-around health of the individual. In short, he states that physical health is not only the product of disciplined spiritual living, but is conducive to spiritual health. For example, the person who sees himself as a vehicle of the Holy Spirit will want to keep the vehicle in good working order, because he knows that a sluggish body is as big a drag on spiritual sharpness as a sluggish engine is a deterrent to good fuel consumption. At the same time, increasing spiritual awareness of the wonder of God's creation will lead the reverent soul to more deeply appreciate the intricacies of his body and refuse more determinedly to allow anything to destroy it, other than the natural processes of change that ultimately lead to death and a new body like Christ's glorious body.

For these reasons a healthy attitude to physical exertion is necessary. The Proverbs speak loudly and long about the merits of good old-fashioned hard work, both praising the consequences of it and warning of the consequences of avoiding it. "As vinegar to the teeth and smoke to the eyes, so is a sluggard to those who send him" (Proverbs 10:26) is a striking condemnation of the lazy person, whereas "He who works his land will have abundant food, but he who chases fantasies lacks judgment" (Proverbs 12:11) is a ringing endorsement of the values, material and otherwise, of honest hard work. In Solomon's days only a small band of the ultrawealthy could afford not to work hard in physical terms, and so it went without saying that those who worked hard would stand a better chance of some degree of financial well-being. Living, as we do, in the days of automation and sedentary occupation, we cannot assume that hard work will bring physical reward, because in actuality it may produce exactly the opposite. Long hours of stress spent sitting in closed environments with short breaks for working luncheons followed by frustrating, tension-packed hours on the freeway systems of the nation are not conducive to good health. The constant demands for increased productivity, the shrill insistence of customers who demand satisfaction yesterday, the all-pervading atmosphere of pressure and tension are producing people both physically depleted and psychologically drained. Paul's words should be heeded, "Physical training is of some value, but godliness has value for all things, holding promise for both the present life and the life to come" (1 Timothy 4:8).

At first sight it might appear that Paul was rather grudging in his support of physical exercise, but the emphasis at this point of his letter to Timothy was spiritual well-being which pays eternal dividends rather than physical fitness which, of course, pays temporal dividends. Paul clearly advocated both.

To those who wish to be whole persons, I would urge careful consideration of the relationship of physical health to all other aspects of personhood, and then I would encourage a realistic, disciplined approach to diet, exercise, and rest so that they might enjoy health to the body and nourishment to the bones.

When we turn our attention to wealth, we recognize that we are dealing with something very dear to most people's hearts. Those who have it are deeply concerned about using it and losing it, and those who don't have it are often intensely interested in acquiring it and enjoying it. But why is wealth so important? To most people wealth means independence. They can do what they want to do. Given enough money they believe just about everything and perhaps anybody is available to them, because "every man has his price." Wealth, therefore, opens up vistas of power and enjoyment that delight the imaginations of those who enjoy such things or aspire to them. There is a sense in which people who have money feel secure. If they become ill they feel they can get the best doctor money can buy. If they become disabled they have enough invested to be able to survive comfortably, and if worse should come to worse and the economy should crash or the Communists take over, they can always get their money out and live somewhere else! To be in a position where money can buy security, happiness, independence, and power is to be where many people would give their eyeteeth to be, so it is no wonder that so many people are so interested in wealth.

So far we have thought about what money can do, and incidentally this is as far as most people want to go when they consider money. But what is money? As human beings we have only so many years to live, so much energy to expend, so many skills to develop, and so many opportunities to take. The result of these years spent in developing and marketing skills with all the strength we can muster in the opportunities that come our way is, to put it bluntly, wealth. To a marked degree, therefore, our wealth or lack of it is a reflection of the ways in which we have used the time, skill, energy, and opportunity with which we have been blessed. In many ways it is possible to learn something about a person through his wealth, because it may be an indication of his triumph over adversity, his remarkable ability to market an idea, his devotion to an ideal, or simply unmistakable evidence of blood, sweat, and tears. In this sense wealth is an extension of ourselves. It is not so much something we have as something we are. Let me at this point stress, however, that I carefully listed "opportunity" as a factor, because as we all recognize, there are wealthy people who were born with a silver spoon in their mouths and are too lazy to take it out, and there are poor people who are brilliant but have never been able to break out of the ghetto of their environment or the disabilities with which they have been afflicted.

If our wealth is a reflection of what we are, the way we handle it will demonstrate this even more clearly than the way we amass it. The Old Testament insisted that wealth should be shared, and that the sharing would be not only evidence of compassion for those less fortunate, but more importantly an indication of love and respect for the Lord. This may be hard for people to grasp if only because we rarely think in these terms. But if we remember that wealth is the product of the time and opportunities, the gifts and the strength that have been given to us as gifts, we should readily appreciate our wealth as fundamentally being the product of the unsolicited gifts with which we have been provided. To take these raw materials and use them to produce for ourselves, without acknowledging the Lord in sharing the produce, is discourteous to say the least and downright arrogant to be honest. Accordingly, from earliest times, the people of God learned to express appreciation for blessings received by making offerings to the Lord. This is what it means to "honor the Lord."

It is interesting to note that Solomon impressed upon his readers that they should offer the first fruits of their wealth to the Lord. The situation in his day was quite different from ours in that paper money, with all its mixed blessings, had not arrived on the scene, so wealth was amassed and transferred in kind. Someone might trade a goat for a knife, rather like someone I heard on my first visit to America trying to trade a monkey for a gun on a radio program called "Swap 'n' Shop." To offer to the Lord, therefore, did not mean to write a pledge or pop something in the plate. It meant when the farmer reaped his crop, he gave part of the crop to the representatives of the Lord, and it is important to remember that he gave the very first sheaf, or the first lamb, or the first load of olives, hence the expression "first fruits." The reason for the necessity of first fruits was that they had to show they held the Lord in high regard by giving to him first, because that was his position in their lives. Practical considerations, no doubt, contributed to this idea as well, because they, like us, might have been tempted to see how big the harvest was before they gave some of it away, but this was ruled out by the law of first fruits. Their giving, therefore, was a step of faith and a powerful testimony to the fact that they had learned to do what Solomon had taught them, "Trust in the LORD with all your heart and lean not on your own understanding; in all your ways acknowledge him, and he will make your paths straight" (Proverbs 3:5, 6).

There was a further aspect of wealth that Solomon expounded. He taught that in the degree in which they acknowledged God's hand of blessing upon them in their giving, so God would further give to them. This, of course, was a great incentive to them to give, but as their history clearly shows it was not always an incentive because as their spiritual vitality waned so their giving decreased. There is a sense in which it is generally true that the Lord gives as we give and material blessing is the product of careful attention to spiritual life and an evidence of God's hand of blessing upon us, but it must not be regarded as a rule without exception. Jesus, himself, was a poor man having at times no place to lay his head and on at least one occasion not enough money to pay his taxes. He lived frugally and simply, eschewing many of the comforts of life and using many fierce words of condemnation to those who were wrapped up in their wealth. Many of God's choicest people, whom I have met around the world, have been careful to "honor the Lord," but because of their circumstances either through political oppression or the

economic condition of their country, have been far
from wealthy. Then, of course, we should not use the
American way of life as the standard of normality.
When I spoke to a group of pastors in Zambia some
years ago, I was amazed to discover that most of the
pastors had walked to the conference for many days,
but one or two of the wealthy men had ridden their
bicycles! "A good name is more desirable than great
riches; to be esteemed is better than silver or gold.
Rich and poor have this in common: The LORD is the
Maker of them all" (Proverbs 22:1, 2). The principle,
however, holds true as the Lord is pleased to supply
the needs of his people and give them a surplus so
they might enjoy his good things and have the joy of
giving from their abundance.

We should always bear in mind that in the same
way the Lord allows some people who live and serve
him to live in relative poverty, he also, for reasons
known only to himself, allows some people who are
opposed to him to prosper, in temporal terms, as we
can see from Solomon's reminder, "A fortune made
from a lying tongue is a fleeting vapor and a deadly
snare" (Proverbs 21:6) and "Dishonest money dwindles away, but he who gathers money little by little
makes it grow" (Proverbs 13:11). These proverbs also
remind us that there is a terrible possibility money
may be abused not only by those who gain it wrong-
fully, but by those who may have been blessed by the
Lord in terms of wealth, but have failed to respond
in giving as they have been encouraged. There has
always been a tendency for people to be greedy, and

this selfish trait is most often demonstrated in the unwillingness of those who have been blessed materially to share that with which they have been blessed. Solomon was particularly anxious to impress this unpalatable truth upon his readers, for many of them appeared to be unaware that the day was coming when either they would leave their money or their money would leave them. It "dwindles away" and is "a fleeting vapor" and "Be sure you know the condition of your flocks, give careful attention to your herds; for riches do not endure forever, and a crown is not secure for all generations" (Proverbs 27:23, 24). With this in mind it behooves everyone who has wealth of any kind to evaluate what they have done with it before they arrive at the place where it has been eaten up by inflation or excess, or they have become so selfishly motivated that they cannot bear to share what they have.

A few days ago when skimming through a best-selling book on money, I was discouraged to discover that while there were chapters relating to every aspect of money, including how to make money, how to invest money, how to gain money from inflation, how to earn more money, how to save money, there was no chapter, or mention of how to give money away. Perhaps that in itself is a striking commentary on our contemporary world. Remember "He who gives to the poor will lack nothing, but he who closes his eyes to them receives many curses" (Proverbs 28:27).

No one, to the best of my knowledge, had a better

understanding of the potential of money for destruction than Agur, who wrote a number of the proverbs found in Scripture. His heartfelt prayer to the Lord says it all: "Two things I ask of you, O LORD: do not refuse me before I die: Keep falsehood and lies far from me; give me neither poverty nor riches, but give me only my daily bread. Otherwise, I may have too much and disown you and say, 'Who is the LORD?' Or I may become poor and steal and so dishonor the name of my God" (Proverbs 30:7–9).

SIX

Straight Talk About Sex

I am my lover's and my lover is mine.

Song of Solomon 6:3

All societies are confronted with the need to control sexual expression for the good of the society, and yet to give freedom for adequate sexual experience for the good of the people. The need to control sexual activity to some degree is easily recognized when we look at the sexual potency of the average male. He has the physical capabilities of producing enough sperm in his lifetime to populate our planet five hundred times. Fortunately, there are other restrictive factors which make this an impossibility, nevertheless, it is obvious that the sexual capabilities of man have to be governed by considerations other than physical ability. Many societies, grappling with soaring birthrates and diminishing resources, are looking for all manner of means to control the products of man's sexuality. The general concern felt for earth's capabilities to support an escalating population speak forcibly to the relative failure of many of these efforts.

Horrifying solutions have been put forth by various science fiction writers which are not taken too seriously; and other, not quite so terrifying but equally disturbing, suggestions are being made by responsible people in positions to implement their ideas. Tampering with family structures, altering marital relationships, enforcing sterilization, providing abortion opportunities and many other ideas are being propagated, all with a view to controlling man's powerful sexuality. Unfortunately, however, most of the solutions violate, in one way or another, the freedom that man must have to exercise his sexuality in order to function normally.

With such a major force as the human sexual potential and such powerful consequences resulting from the exercise of this force worrying our contemporary society, it is comforting to note that the Bible is not silent on the subject. It is also exciting to see that included in the wisdom of Proverbs is a considerable amount of frank and realistic talk about human sexuality, which is particularly surprising when one recognizes that the church, which professes to operate on the basis of the book, has so often been much more reluctant to speak to the subject than the book itself. In fact, the Bible has been so outspoken on the subject of sex that some of its readers have had to turn some pages very quickly, and many of its preachers and teachers have found it necessary to carefully avoid large pieces of its teaching when working through its pages.

Starting right at the beginning of Scripture, in the

story of Creation, we are introduced to the inescapable truth that God is the creator of sexuality. For reasons that are perfectly obvious, God intended the sexuality of "man, male and female," whom He had created, to be employed not only in the reproductive process for the development and population of the earth in which man had been placed as the divine agent, but also for the mutual satisfaction and delight which husband and wife needed and which God intended they should possess. This is clearly demonstrated in the loneliness of man without woman and the sheer delight with which man greeted his counterpart. Although the Hebrew is not totally clear to us in our English versions when Adam saw Eve for the first time, he shouted something like, "At last . . . !" It is equally fascinating to remember the very earliest statements of Scripture show that man and woman are to live together in a relationship which is so united that "they will become one flesh" (Genesis 2:24). This, of course, shows that in the original design man and woman were to be mutually committed and mutually supportive in every dimension of their being, including the uniting of their physical beings as the term "one flesh" clearly intimates.

As time went on and it was necessary for the Lord to make known to his people some working principles, he gave the instructions through Moses which we commonly call the Ten Commandments. The first four commandments are all related to man's relationship to God and the last six deal with man's relationships with man. It is noteworthy that half the instructions relating to interpersonal relationships pay particular attention to human sexuality. "Honor your father and mother. . . . You shall not commit adultery. . . . You shall not covet your neighbor's wife . . . " (Exodus 20:12–17). The biblical concern with human sexuality is clearly expressed, and it is important that the biblical view be clearly understood in the debate that rages on the subject at the present time.

There are two main concerns in the Scriptures regarding sex. The first is a concern related to sexual activity outside the confines of marital commitment, and the second relates to inadequate sexual expression within the bonds of matrimony. The abuse of sex outside of marriage has led to innumerable problems, as has the inadequate sexual experience of many married couples. Solomon had trenchant words to say to both situations. "For the lips of an adulteress drip honey, and her speech is smoother than oil; but in the end she is bitter as gall, sharp as a double-edged sword" (Proverbs 5:3, 4).

Solomon's strong statements sound strange in today's world where so much sweet-talking about extramarital sex is the norm. But we should not forget his own experience. As Matthew recorded the genealogy of Christ, he made no bones about the situation when he wrote, "David was the father of Solomon, whose mother had been Uriah's wife" (Matthew 1:6). King David had committed adultery with Bathsheba, the wife of Uriah, while her husband was away fighting for the king. She became pregnant; David panicked. All kinds of maneuvering took place which resulted in Uriah's being killed at David's command. God sent his prophet Nathan to rebuke David for his sin and to alert him to the consequences. Subsequently, the baby born only survived seven days and grief piled on grief. No doubt Solomon was aware of this episode in the life of his own father and mother before they were married to each other. He knew at firsthand the pain and grief, the deceit and humiliation which had accompanied the adulterous relationship, so he had no problem contrasting the sweetness of the moments passed in a lover's arms with the bitterness that inevitably resulted.

No doubt David and Bathsheba could have made a good case for their relationship if they had wished to view it in purely humanistic terms. He was bored and needed some excitement—she was lonely and needed some company. Her husband was away and she had needs that she could reasonably expect to be fulfilled—he was a king and afforded her the chance of a little glamour in an otherwise drab, lonely existence. Anyway, Uriah need never know, and they didn't intend to hurt anybody, so why not? On top of all that, she was extremely beautiful and appeared wonderfully available, and he was very famous and offered all kinds of possibilities. The pull was enormous from both sides. But the shame that both felt eventually was not only that they had been unfaithful to Uriah and deceived this dedicated man, even taken his life, but they had violated a divine principle of which they were both fully aware. As David wrote later, "Have mercy on me, O God, according to Your unfailing love; according to Your great compassion blot out my transgressions . . . . Against You, You only have I sinned and done what is evil in Your sight" (Psalms 51:1–4). Adultery, according to the Scripture, is certainly attractive because of the immediate pleasure it offers and the sense of freedom and glamour it brings. "She took hold of him and kissed him and with a brazen face she said: I have peace offerings at home; today I fulfilled my vows. So I came out to meet you; I looked for you and have found you! I have covered my bed with colored linens from Egypt. I have perfumed my bed with myrrh, aloes, and cinnamon. Come, let's drink deep of love till morning; let's enjoy ourselves with love! My husband is not at home; he has gone on a long journey. He took his purse filled with money and will not be home till full moon" (Proverbs 7:13–20). But it is contrary to all that God has in mind for the human race, which he has ordained should be nurtured in families that are based on stable, loving marriages. To undermine the marriage bond through adultery is to strike at the root of the family unit, which ultimately is to erode the stability of society itself. According to divine principle, it is as serious as that!

In recent years it has been socially acceptable for people to disregard such niceties as marriage, and more and more people have been enjoying the benefits of conjugal rights and privileges without finding it necessary to legalize what they were doing. When shown this, they have usually pointed out that they see no necessity for a "piece of paper" which says they can go to bed together, and as they are mature people and have a good working relationship, they see no necessity for marriage. At the time of writing this book, a most interesting turn of events has taken place. In the celebrated "Marvin versus Marvin" case in California, Ms. Marvin, who had lived for a number of years with the actor Lee Marvin without the benefit of wedlock and was subsequently discarded, had sued the actor for half his earnings while they lived together. To put it mildly, her action had a lot of people running for the bushes, and although she didn't get what she wanted, she did manage to shake the community, which now advises people who intend to live together without marriage to "have an understanding in writing" before they ever get into bed! The question that many of us who have stood firmly for the marriage bond and the principle of mutual commitment want answered now is, "What is the difference between the 'piece of paper' which you denigrated and the 'understanding in writing' that is now advocated?"

Many a man hit with alimony, or "palimony," would have been well-advised to heed Solomon, who said, "Keep to a path far from her, do not go near the door of her house, lest you give your best strength to others and your years to one who is cruel, lest strangers feast on your wealth and your toil enrich another man's house" (Proverbs 5:8–10). Solomon's

advice to the men of his day was perfectly straightforward, and while many modern women take exception to his emphasis which appears to place the
blame for adultery on "the fairer sex," we should not
allow this specific cultural aspect of his writing to
distract us from the basic principles he was enjoining.
Today's society is so different in its understanding of
sexual roles. Its commitment to an egalitarian life-
style means that both men and women need to be
alert to the possible seductive attitudes of the opposite sex and the necessity for the correct kind of discipline as taught in Scripture. At this point it may not
be out of order to remind ourselves that adultery
need not be confined to heterosexual relationships,
because in today's confused sexual scene, there is
much sad evidence of sexual infidelity in the gay
scene. Solomon's prescription was based on the old
adage that "prevention is better than cure." His
strong advice to those who recognized their own sus-
ceptibility to seduction was, "Keep to a path far from
her, do not go near the door of her house" (Proverbs
5:8). And his wise rhetorical questions, "Can a man
scoop fire into his lap without his clothes being
burned? Can a man walk on hot coals without his feet
being scorched?" (Proverbs 6:27, 28), clearly advo-
cate the necessity for disciplined withdrawal from
and rejection of situations where the temptation may
be more than can be handled.

Joseph is one of the greatest illustrations of a man
who had every opportunity to avail himself of the
excitement of an amorous woman and yet turned her

down because he believed that although the opportunity was obviously attractive and, from a purely pragmatic point of view, expedient, it was quite out of order for him, and he left in a hurry, losing not only his shirt, but also his liberty in the process. I'm sure if he had been interviewed about his decision at a later date, he would not have hesitated to say that, given the same set of circumstances, he would do the same thing!

Because the Bible takes such a strong stand on the subject of sexual abuse, its critics have unjustly and inaccurately accused it of being anti-sexual. The charge has stuck in the thinking of many people and has been applied to all who hold the Bible to be authoritative. It is easy to answer by simply turning the critics' attention to many passages of Scripture which, far from being anti-sexual, are refreshingly frank and helpful on the subject. Proverbs is one of the best examples of this positive approach.

In marked contrast to the adulterous relationships which were so prevalent in Solomon's time and which plague our times, the instruction to husbands was and is: "Drink water from your own cistern, running water from your own well. Should your springs overflow in the streets, your streams of water in the public squares? Let them be yours alone, never to be shared with strangers. May your fountain be blessed, and may you rejoice in the wife of your youth" (Proverbs 5:15–18). The emphasis on "your own" which dominates this passage should not be overlooked because it is the key to understanding the relationship of man and wife. If in these verses it appears rather one-sided (in the man's favor) the imbalance, if it exists, is rectified in the Song of Solomon, where the expressions "My lover is mine and I am his" (Song of Solomon 2:16) and "I am my lover's and my lover is mine" (Song of Solomon 6:3) clearly state the mutuality of commitment which is the basis of the marriage relationship.

It is the subject of commitment which needs to be addressed more than any other in the contemporary sexual debate. The word "love" which is so inextricably bound up in the experience of sex and the relationship of marriage is rarely seen as another word for commitment. "To fall in love" is to have an experience of ecstacy that can make a strong person tremble, a disciplined person forgetful, and a rational person goofy. It makes violins play and eyes sparkle, champagne flow and flowers to bloom. "To make love" is in many instances to engage in sexual intimacies with people who are casual acquaintances at best, and total strangers at worst. In other words, the word "love" has been dreadfully devaluated. Even where marriages have been founded on "love," it is not uncommon to be told that "we fell out of love" or "he doesn't love me anymore, so I feel no necessity to love him." To talk like this is to forget or ignore the fact that loving is committing. To love is not primarily to gain, but to give. Psychologists are practically unanimous in their insistence that some of the greatest needs of the human being are to love and be loved, and one of the greatest causes of immature behavior and inadequate emotional balance is the lack of love. But the love of which they speak is not "making love" or "falling in love." They do not mean by this that "making love" is the basis of strong emotional health or that the absence of "falling in love" is the cause of emotional disturbance. They mean, frankly, that the person who feels that no one is committed to him and that he is committed to no one knows that no one loves him, and that is desperately debilitating. He is dreadfully alone in a big world.

However, where two people come together on the basis of a loving, mutual commitment they enrich each other immeasurably. By this commitment they say, in effect, "You are a person of great worth and inestimable value to me. I commit myself to being what you need. I assure you that your fulfillment is my greatest concern and your enrichment is my deepest desire." To be told that kind of thing by someone whom you feel is very special is to be invited to respond in the same way. Imagine the delight of two people discovering they feel that the other is worth protecting and encouraging, supporting and nurturing! This is the stuff of which marriages are made and families are built.

The biblical view of sex is that, given this approach of mutual commitment called "love," there should of necessity be a physical demonstration of this mutuality. God made male and female wonderfully capable of expressing the sense of assurance and abandonment which comes from an understanding of the other person's commitment. This abandonment is shown to greatest effect in the ecstacy of the sex act and the fulfillment of the sexual union. However, where the sex act is divorced from the commitment attitude, the very act is a hollow charade of that which it professes to portray. This does not mean, of course, that under such conditions sexual delight is impossible. But it does mean that sex has been wrenched out of context, and that the participants are enjoying with their bodies that which they deny in their minds and refuse with their wills. They may be giving their bodies, but they are not committing themselves.

While it is true that there has been much abuse of sex outside of marriage, it is equally true that much sexual experience within marriage leaves an awful lot to be desired. If the knowledge of commitment stimulates an attitude of abandonment, how on earth can "happily married" people refuse to express this abandonment in sexual ecstasy? I know, of course, that tiredness is a great reason (excuse?) and that busyness is a contributing factor, but when it comes down to the bottom line, the tiredness and the busyness are reflections of an attitude that says a lot of other things are more important than the exercise of sexuality. Paul (the much maligned Paul, that is) wrote, "The husband should fulfill his marital duty to his wife, and likewise the wife to her husband. The wife's body does not belong to her alone but also to her husband. In the same way, the husband's body does not belong to him alone but also to his wife. Do not deprive each other except by mutual consent and for a time, so that you may devote yourselves to prayer. Then come together again so that Satan will not tempt you because of your lack of self-control" (1 Corinthians 7:3–5).

If Paul makes it sound a little bit like fulfilling a rather onerous chore, I am sure this was not his intention, but to many couples sex has become a chore, because they have allowed themselves to degenerate into physically unattractive people whose physical unattractiveness is a reflection of their boring, uninteresting character. Where is the stimulating conversation of the early dates, the rapt attention to the other's every word? What ever happened to the planned surprises and the sparkling reactions? And what of the early joys of intimacies shared and discoveries made? They have gone down the drain of time and left in their place is little but the sludge of mediocrity and the debris of once fertile experience. But this does not happen in Solomon's book. This is not the intent of God for the sexual beings he has made. Mark carefully the words of Scripture: "May your fountain be blessed, and may you rejoice in the wife of your youth. A loving doe, a graceful deer— may her breasts satisfy you always, may you ever be captivated by her love. Why be captivated, my son, by an adulteress? Why embrace the bosom of another man's wife?" (Proverbs 5:18–20). Why indeed?

SEVEN

Forewarned Is Forearmed

*How long will you lie there, you sluggard?
When will you get up from your sleep? A
little sleep, a little slumber, a little folding
of the hands to rest—and poverty will
come on you like a bandit and scarcity like
an armed man.* Proverbs 6:9–11

I am profoundly grateful for the early upbringing
I received. My parents were committed to Christ and
endeavored to introduce me, in early days, not only
to his love but also to the principles of the Word of
God. Not that I always appreciated either my parents' wishes or the scriptural principles they taught.
I remember vividly being extremely resentful when
my father quoted, "Let another praise you, and not
your own mouth; someone else and not your own
lips" (Proverbs 27:2). It seemed to me at the time that
I was justified in being rather proud of what I had
achieved. With the passing of years, however, I have
learned that my dad was right, because my appreciation of my own achievements was, at that time,
rather strident, and the volume of my own voice was
in danger of drowning the value of my own success.
Around the same time I became particularly

friendly with a young couple who lived close to my home. Perhaps my friendship was not altogether unrelated to the fact that they had purchased one of those exciting new toys called in England "the telly." I became such a close friend that I spent more time in their home than in my own. This prompted my mother to remind me, "If you find honey, eat just enough—too much of it and you will vomit. Seldom set foot in your neighbor's house—too much of you, and he will hate you" (Proverbs 25:16, 17).

Then there was the time that I was having some real problems controlling my temper. I was greatly troubled by this evidence of my own immaturity, but my consternation was considerably deepened when I read, "For as churning the milk produces butter, and as twisting the nose produces blood, so stirring up anger produces strife" (Proverbs 30:33).

In each of these incidents, and many more too numerous to mention, I was warned by Scripture of the dangers of my behavior, but instead of being grateful for the warning, initially I resented it. Because this reaction is not uncommon, some of us have failed in our duty as responsible members of society in that we have failed to give adequate warning when it was most necessary.

On one occasion when I endeavored to alert a fellow motorist to the fact that his exhaust pipe had rusted through and was dragging on the ground producing a lot of smoke and sparks, he jumped out of his car and threatened me with a fate much worse than death if I blew my horn at him one more time.

My reaction was to shrug my injured shoulders and say to myself, "Next time, I'll keep my horn shut!"

At the considerable risk of raising some more indignation, I am going to present a variety of warnings from the sixth chapter of Proverbs. Fully realizing that, like most warnings, they may be as unwelcome as they are unsought, I'm going to point them out anyway!

The first warning is the danger that can result from ill-considered kindness. Solomon visualizes a situation where a kindhearted person may have been deeply moved by the plight of a friend or acquaintance, and with considerably more generosity than wisdom, pledged support and help. After this great act of benevolence the kind man discovers, to his horror, that he is unable to deliver what he has promised, and what is more, he may be taken to the brink of ruin by his magnanimity. The advice is surprisingly strong. "Go and humble yourself; press your plea with your neighbor! Allow no sleep to your eyes, no slumber to your eyelids. Free yourself, like a gazelle from the hand of the hunter, like a bird from the snare of the fowler" (Proverbs 6:3–5). Hebrew scholars point out that the words translated "humble yourself" and "press your plea" are exceedingly strong words meaning that decisive action must be taken. The impact of the instruction is intensified by the additional statements found later in Solomon's writings: "Do not be a man who strikes hands in pledge or puts up security for debts; if you lack the means to pay, your very bed will be snatched from under you" (Proverbs 22:26, 27).

It is of the utmost importance that these instructions be weighed carefully against other equally powerful statements of Scripture. The psalmist, for instance, reminds us, "Good will come to him who is generous and lends freely, who conducts his affairs with justice" (Psalms 112:5). To this must be added Solomon's own positive statements, "He who is kind to the poor lends to the LORD, and he will reward him for what he has done" (Proverbs 19:17); and, "He who gives to the poor will lack nothing, but he who closes his eyes to them receives many curses" (Proverbs 28:27).

Kindness and generosity are Christian virtues which need to be constantly demonstrated by those who profess to be disciples of him who gave himself for our redemption. Paul, with beautiful simplicity, put it this way: "For you know the grace of our Lord Jesus Christ that though he was rich, yet for your sakes he became poor, so that you through his poverty might become rich" (2 Corinthians 8:9). There can be no suggestion, therefore, in this warning of Solomon that believers should hang on to all that they have, and if they have offered to help anyone who is experiencing difficulty they should immediately extricate themselves. The thrust of this passage is not to encourage selfishness, but to insist on sensible kindness. It is not particularly beneficial for people in need to be proffered help by those who are unable to deliver, any more than it is particularly commendable for those who cannot help to act as though they could. It is the action that comes from those whose hearts rule their heads that is condemned.

As a pastor I have found that it is extremely difficult to say "no" to some people in some circumstances. They, quite rightly, have been led to believe that someone who has devoted his life to the ministry of Christ can reasonably be expected to help, but what they don't understand sometimes is that the help they desire would, in the long run, be more like a hindrance. There is a certain pressure that can almost amount to spiritual blackmail, which is applied to those who serve Christ as his disciples; and to this pressure many have succumbed to their own detriment and the loss of those they most wished to help. Be warned about the necessity of saying "no" if saying "yes" would be easier but not necessarily better. Have the moral courage to do that which is unpopular, if doing that which is popular would end up being less than beneficial.

The second item on Solomon's list of warnings is easier to understand, although the suggestion that we might need the warning will be no easier to take. The first warning was against ill-considered kindness, the second talks about ill-fated laziness. Even the most cursory glance at Solomon's life-style will show that he was an extremely able and gifted man, whose energy seems to have matched his gift. His feats in government were legendary, for during his lifetime, "Judah and Israel, from Dan to Beersheba, lived in

safety, each man under his own vine and fig tree"
(1 Kings 4:25). The task of building the superb Temple which took seven years was only surpassed by the
undertaking to build his own palace, which required
thirteen years. He built all manner of remarkable
buildings, restored damaged sites, terraced the city
of David, built the walls of Megiddo and other cities,
and found time to establish a navy and develop trade
over a wide area. All this on top of his studies! There
was probably not a single lazy bone in his body. This
only led him to recognize the dangers of laziness and
speak out against it, "How long will you lie there, you
sluggard? When will you get up from your sleep? A
little sleep, a little slumber, a little folding of the
hands to rest—and poverty will come on you like a
bandit, and scarcity like an armed man" (Proverbs
6:9–11). The lazy man doesn't intend to be lazy, it's
just that he doesn't have any great motivation to be,
or do, anything. He doesn't make monumental decisions to adopt a life-style of indolence, he simply can't
be bothered to think about a life-style. It is all done
"little by little." Just another few minutes' sleep, a
few more moments' delay. There's no hurry or emer-
gency, no sense of the necessary or feeling for the
obligatory. Just a little less of this and not quite so
much of that. The insidious nature of laziness is marvelously portrayed in these words of Solomon: "As a
door turns on its hinges, so a sluggard turns on his
bed" (Proverbs 26:14). The dangerous aspect is also
clearly sketched. The "bandit" and the "armed man"
are presumably related to the "thief" of which our

more modern proverb speaks. "Procrastination is the thief of time." The dissipation of opportunity and the waste of ability are possibly two of the most shameful things about laziness. Solomon certainly made this point even if he needed just a touch of exaggeration to achieve it! "The sluggard buries his hand in the dish; he is too lazy to bring it back to his mouth" (Proverbs 26:15). In all fairness to this lazy individual, however, we must say that he had at least taken the trouble to make the meal, even if the effort left him too exhausted to eat it! This is more than can be said for his idle friend described as follows: "The lazy man does not roast his game, but the diligent man prizes his possession" (Proverbs 12:27). Lazy people, however, don't take kindly to having their particular aversion to activity pointed out. They are inclined to think that their laziness is an indication of their superiority. Anybody can hack out a living, but it takes an unusual person to survive by the use of things other than sweat and energy, work and labor. "The sluggard is wiser in his own eyes than seven men who answer discreetly" (Proverbs 26:16). And if he cannot convince his critics of his imagined superiority he will probably be particularly adept at presenting excuses for his inactivity: "The sluggard will not plow by reason of the cold" (Proverbs 20:4 KJV); or real or imaginary obstacles preclude him from the activity: "The sluggard says, 'There is a lion outside! I will be murdered in the streets!'" (Proverbs 22:13). Whatever the excuses or the reasons, the laziness of the lazy man will make him a burden to society as well as to his family, but more than that he will be guilty of a wasted life.

Because the early chapters of Genesis, which speak of the fall of man, record the curse of God in the words, "Cursed is the ground because of you; through painful toil you will eat of it all the days of your life. It will produce thorns and thistles for you and you will eat the plants of the field. By the sweat of your brow you will eat your food . . . " (Genesis 3:17–19), some people have been led to believe that work is a curse. They have not read the Scripture very carefully or they would have seen that man was made to work in his perfect state, that God worked and enjoyed what he was doing, that Jesus worked in glad obedience to the Father, and that those whom Christ chose as his disciples were men who were not afraid of getting their hands dirty. The drudgery of work is the result of man's downfall, not work itself. It is man's fallen attitude to his work that makes him so dissatisfied, so disgruntled and so difficult.

The believer in Christ recognizes that, while work will be hard and circumstances difficult because he lives in a fallen world populated by a fallen humanity, his work has, nevertheless, great importance. The way he does his work, in itself, can be that which brings glory to God. And not only that, the way he works is going to determine to some extent how well he is able to fulfill his obligations not only to his employer but also to his family. Paul's comment, "If a man will not work, he shall not eat" (2 Thessalonians 3:10), needs no explanation! And his marvelous instruction, "He who has been stealing must steal no longer, but must work, doing something useful with his hands, that he may have something to share with those in need" (Ephesians 4:28), reminds us that the beauty of honest work is that it provides the worker with which to help people in need. The lazy man has no productivity and, accordingly, becomes a burden on society. Instead of being the means of help to those with real need, he cloaks his own laziness in a robe of pseudoneed and not only fails to meet real need but takes from those who ought to be helped. The lazy man, therefore, is a disgrace to his race, a burden to his society, a disappointment to his family, and a drain on the resources available to the genuinely needy. Solomon said succinctly, "One who is slack in his work is brother to one who destroys" (Proverbs 18:9) and pungently, "As vinegar to the teeth and smoke to the eyes, so is a sluggard to those who send him" (Proverbs 10:26).

Finally in the list of warnings we come to Solomon's dire words concerning ill-concealed guiltiness. To him, there was a particularly unpleasant aspect to the life-style of people who went about not only sinning, but doing it with a casual, almost belligerent air, as if challenging God to do something about it. The Word of God says unequivocally such a person had better be warned that one of these days God will accept the challenge and deal with his wickedness. "A scoundrel and villain, who goes about with a corrupt mouth, who winks with his eye, signals with his feet and motions with his fingers, who plots evil with deceit in his heart—he always stirs up dissension. Therefore disaster will overtake him in an instant; he will suddenly be destroyed—without remedy" (Proverbs 6:12–15).

There is a dangerous and common misconception about God which views him as being so benevolent and loving, and perhaps lenient and even forgetful, that whatever else he may or may not do, he will never judge anybody. This view flies defiantly in the teeth of the explicit teaching of Scripture and is more the product of wishful thinking than rational thought. It ought to be obvious that we are responsible to our society for the things we do. The whole of the judicial system operates on the premise of human accountability and responsibility. Further, it allows for the fact that responsibility and accountability demand that proper punishment for crime be applied and adequate retribution for misdemeanors be administered. To fail to do this is to deny the responsibility of the person concerned. It makes him something less than a viable person, more like a meaningless machine governed by factors bigger and greater than himself. To insist on retribution and responsibility is to hold man high as a moral agent, whose actions are significant because he himself is significant. This being the case, it should not be too difficult for us to accept and admit that if God exists, the greatest compliment he can pay an individual is to tell him that his actions and being are so significant he will be held responsible for them.

Men engage in actions, for which they are responsible, that are totally contrary not only to God's instructions but, more importantly, to God's very nature and purpose. And God hates this: "There are six things the LORD hates, seven that are detestable to him: haughty eyes, a lying tongue, hands that shed innocent blood, a heart that devises wicked schemes, feet that are quick to rush into evil, a false witness who pours out lies and a man who stirs up dissension among brothers" (Proverbs 6:16–19). To be told that God "hates" things may sound rather strange to some of us, because we either don't think of God having such feelings or we can't quite see why he should be so upset. We feel rather like the little boy sent to his room for misbehaving with his mother's scolding words reverberating in his ears, "God will be angry with you for being so bad." Shortly after arriving in his room, there develops a major storm, and the chastened mother creeps upstairs to see how her son is reacting. He is standing by the window, watching the lightning and listening to the crashing thunder, saying, "All right God, I know you're angry, but aren't you overreacting just a little?"

The fact is that God is not overreacting, but that we are underestimating the reality of sin and the immensity of our guilt.

The "haughty eyes" which he hates are the projectors of pride. Pride is the most heinous of things, because it usurps God's position and accepts for itself accolades and recognitions which are his by right. Pride, therefore, is basically the denial of deity by frail humanity and the assumption of divinity by sinful mankind.

The "lying tongue" is the instrument that projects error, aims to deceive, and denies truth. God operates in exactly the opposite direction, as he seeks to bring people to a knowledge of the Truth so they can be delivered from the agonies of error and liberated from the excesses of confusion.

The "hands that shed innocent blood," of course, are murderous hands which, in taking another life, deny the "image of God" in which man is made and insult God by lowering man to the level of meaningless animal.

"The heart that devises wicked schemes" majors in craftiness and deceitfulness. These are things that God hates, because they are carefully designed to trick people out of their rightful position and possessions, and anyone who thinks man can be tricked with impunity, doesn't think much of man at all. But God does!

It is not just man's readiness to engage in wrongdoing that upsets God but the enthusiasm with which his "feet . . . are quick to rush into evil." If man were to be dragged screaming and kicking into evil practice, it would at least give the impression that he desired not to do the evil thing and might even be unable to help himself. But this is not the case. All too often, he shows a very definite aptitude for evil. In the same vein, it isn't just that man will lie to cover himself when he is in a tight corner, but he sometimes shows such skill and determination in his distortion of and departure from the truth that his disregard for what is right is painfully apparent. All these and many others lead inevitably to "dissension among brothers," which the Lord hates, because He made man to live in union with Himself and with each other. But from the day sin entered into the world, the man that God loves has shown a bent to things that God hates. This sin is deeply hated because, in addition to ruining the ones who perpetrate it and those against whom it is committed, it is an affront to God's nature. Fortunately Scripture reminds us that sin can be forgiven. The nature of God still allows him to love, with a never-ending love, man whom He made. This love is, of course, demonstrated in the death of Christ for sinners, an event which not only shows starkly and unforgettably the love of God but also God's hatred for sin. If ever we are tempted to doubt his love or condone the sin he hates, a long look at the cross will remind us of the greatness of his love and hate.

As we saw in the first chapter, it was the Romans who first said, "forewarned is forearmed," and their military successes were, no doubt, partly due to the brilliance of their intelligence, which let them know what to expect, and the strength of the army to handle what they expected. In the struggle which we call life, to be forewarned is to be forearmed only when we see in the warning the intentions of God and take from him the forgiveness for past sin and the strength to avoid the same sin in the future.

EIGHT

Where Does the Buck Stop?

On the heights along the way, where the paths meet, she takes her stand.

Proverbs 8:2

We have a special term for evading responsibility. We call it "passing the buck." Ever since God asked Adam what he thought he was doing, "passing the buck" has been a popular pastime. Adam blamed Eve for his misdemeanor and, also rather unsubtly, inferred that the whole nasty business was really God's fault. Eve, not to be outdone, promptly blamed the serpent, who had nobody to blame. But God showed that, wriggle and squirm as they would, his children were responsible.

Philosophically and psychologically, we have come a long way in recent years, and the journey has taken us farther into the woods of "determinism." In a nutshell, this approach to the human condition states that we are what we are because of our unfortunate circumstances, our unsatisfactory environment, our stupid parents, knavish politicians, and errant genes. This is all delightfully heady stuff, but unfortunately the people who profess to believe it don't really believe it themselves. Sometime, while they are propagating their theories, accidentally stand on their toes, and when they tell you not to be so clumsy, point out to them that it was not really your fault, but the fault of the architect who desigened the building, the builder who put it up slightly crooked, the cobbler who made your shoes unbalanced, and the injured party for getting in your way. You will find that, far from feeling it was all determined, they will hold you responsible, and the more you explain that you are the unfortunate victim of all manner of terrible forces, the more frustrated with your endeavors to "pass the buck" they will become! Furthermore, you will find that some of the most famous advocates of determinism have published their views in books, which presumably they expect people to buy, read, believe, and act upon. But if the readers are preconditioned, and their reactions are determined, surely to write a book designed to alter their predetermined reaction must be the greatest exercise in futility!

The man in the street, whoever he may be, doesn't worry about such obscure, abstract considerations. All he knows is that it's easier to blame someone else than to accept the blame himself. So the employer in his oak-panelled boardroom is a sitting duck, the umpire peering through the clouds of dust thrown up by sliding base runners is a myopic fink, and the President for whom he voted two years previously is personally responsible for the Middle East, the cost of living, the weather, and the state of the Democratic Party, not to mention the fall of the Shah, the rise of the yen, the cost of medical care, and the scarcity of gasoline. Of course, the President, when he was campaigning, did say something about the desk in the Oval room having a sign on it which says, "the buck stops here," but ever since he got in the Oval room he seems to have been pushing the buck in the direction of the Congress, Exxon, and the Ayatollah. In short, everybody wants to make sure that he takes as little blame as possible and accepts as little responsibility as is absolutely necessary.

In all fairness, we must admit that the President is not always to blame for what has happened, because however much he may have given the impression when he was campaigning that he had all the answers, everybody knows that he does not have them, and even if he had, he wouldn't necessarily be allowed to put them into action. There are other forces with which to reckon. This is true in all walks of life, so while we must reject the idea that everything is determined by forces beyond our control, and we are, therefore, not responsible, we must be careful not to throw the baby out with the bathwater. There are factors in all our behavior patterns that can be traced to outside forces, but nevertheless we, as human beings, are responsible for our handling of these factors, and we alone must answer for our response to these forces. The President may have his hands tied by the Congress and his plans thwarted by the Russians, but he, while not responsible for either the

Congress or the Russians, is responsible for his handling of both in his capacity as President.

The boy brought up in the ghetto may not be responsible for his father's unemployment, the government's failure to upgrade his neighborhood, and his school's inability to create an environment conducive to learning. He may, therefore, be extremely susceptible to a suggestion that he should make a quick buck through illegitimate activity and have some fun in doing something wrong, which will at least alleviate his boredom. But he is still responsible for his decision to act illegally and to behave wrongly. To suggest that his behavior was not in some way the product of his circumstances would be foolish, but to take the next step and insist that he was not responsible is downright irresponsible, for it not only flies straight into the teeth of biblical teaching, but it also relegates mankind to the level of a machine and banishes him to a moral and ethical wilderness, wherein dwell only the dried-out skeletons of human tragedy and the shrill howls of vicious forces bent on tearing man asunder.

The writer of Proverbs had a great emphasis on the necessity of gaining wisdom, as we have seen so far, but in the eighth chapter he went a step further, and after presenting a superb passage in which wisdom, personfied as a woman, makes a moving appeal, he concluded with the powerful words, "For whoever finds me finds life and receives favor from the LORD. But whoever fails to find me harms himself; all who hate me love death" (Proverbs 8:35, 36). It is abundantly clear from these words that individuals are responsible to find wisdom, that success in the search for it spells "life" and "favor from the Lord," and that failure to find wisdom means the person concerned "harms himself," and may even "love death," if the reason for his failure to discover wisdom can be attributed to his rejection of what God has revealed.

Our generation is characterized by something which at first sight appears to be quite magnificent, but which on deeper reflection is seen to be quite the opposite. I refer to the prevailing attitude of "tolerance." Seen against the background of man's unspeakable atrocities to mankind, most of which have been the products of ideological differences, and many of which have had religious connotations, the emphasis on tolerance shines like a bright ray of hope in a murky scene. No one wants to live again in the days of the Inquisition, the excesses of the Crusades, the horrors of the Holocaust, and the reaction against such things, which is partially responsible for the current state of affairs, is fully understandable. However, as is so often the case, the reaction has produced an overreaction, and we find ourselves in a situation where we are so tolerant that we will tolerate practically anything. This has led to the position where it is popular to allow everyone the right to believe whatever they wish without challenging it, even though this toleration leads us to the ridiculous position of allowing mutually contradictory beliefs to cohabit. Even the most cursory glance at the contem-

porary scene will show that there are some odd bed-
fellows in the world of ideas!

At the risk of stating the obvious, we should point
out that the belief that God exists and the belief that
God does not exist are mutually contradictory. Contemporary tolerance requires that we live peaceably
in an environment where both beliefs have equal
viability and where the believer in each position does
not have the right to challenge the other position.
But, deep down, everybody knows that both views
cannot be right, for even God cannot exist and not
exist at the same time! There has to be, therefore,
what some people call the "intolerance of Truth."
Truth cannot and will not tolerate the opposite of
Truth. Wrong must be opposed by right.

We must, therefore, insist that, while tolerance in
the face of differing opinions is commendable when
it delivers us from harmful attitudes and destructive
actions, the type of tolerance which allows people to
believe error and to make havoc of their lives must
be countered. This is part of the human responsibility because, as Solomon explained, each person is
required to throw off the lethargy of ill-conceived
tolerance and actively discover the truth. "Listen, for
I have worthy things to say; I open my lips to speak
what is right" (Proverbs 8:6).

We are not free to believe wrong when right is
available, any more than we are allowed to teach
error when truth is discoverable. One of the most
disturbing things I have discovered in my pastoral
ministry is people's reluctance to discuss the "right-

ness" of a situation. For instance, a young lady came to see me a few days ago in great distress. She was living with her boss, without the benefit of wedlock, and had become pregnant. Her boyfriend had told her to "get rid of the child," but she said she loved children. Her problem was, therefore, that she wanted to keep what he wanted not to keep. I asked if she had talked to her family, and she answered they had said, "You decide for yourself. Whatever makes you happy is fine with us." Everybody concerned, as far as I could see, had approached the difficult situation from the point of view of what they wanted. The boyfriend wanted to be rid of the child, the girl wanted to have the child, the parents wanted to be left out of the whole business; everybody had one thing in common—they all wanted what they wanted. I asked the young lady if she had stopped thinking about what everybody preferred and given any consideration to what was "right." Her uncomprehending look quickly showed me she had not even considered that there might be a "right" and a "wrong" conclusion to the problem; and her primary responsibility was to discover the right and do it and expose the wrong and avoid it. Ultimately she will be responsible not so much for doing what she or anybody else wanted, but for discovering the rightness of the situation and doing it.

The complexities of modern living are compounded by our failure to accept that there are absolute standards for behavior. With our commendable emphasis on the benefits of a pluralistic society, as stated in the nation motto *E pluribus unum,* we have allowed ourselves to be maneuvered into a state of mind that believes, not so much that there are different ways of arriving at the ultimate Truth but that there is no ultimate Truth, and the different ways are themselves all that is necessary. Solomon would have none of that kind of thinking, as he clearly showed when he wrote about wisdom: "On the heights along the way, where the paths meet, she takes her stand" (Proverbs 8:2). That there are innumerable ways of arriving at the Truth concerning the reality of life must be beyond doubt, as anyone who has listened to people from around the world will readily agree. But that there are numerous truths that are mutually contradictory and yet equally true is a nonsensical attitude all too common. The Christian belief that Christ is what he claimed to be cannot live comfortably with other beliefs that say he was not what he claimed to be. Somebody is wrong about Christ! When he insisted that he was uniquely the Son of God who would rise from the dead, he was either right or wrong. His bold statement that he could give eternal life to all who would receive it from him was either true or false. In addition, religious beliefs which teach that man can get to the Father other than through the Son have to be balanced against his word which stated that, "no man comes to the Father but by me" (*see* John 14:6). Either he was wrong or they are wrong, and each person has the responsibility to find out for himself what the Truth is. Obviously, some people will start at one point and others at a totally different point. Some, because of the accident of their birth, will be exposed to one line of thinking more readily than others, and for these things they are not responsible, but they are responsible to examine the evidence available to them and work assiduously to arrive at the Truth.

This is the unmistakable thrust of the appeal and challenge from the mouth of Wisdom herself, "To you, O men, I call out; I raise my voice to all mankind. You who are simple, gain prudence; you who are foolish, gain understanding . . . . Choose my instruction instead of silver, knowledge rather than choice gold, for wisdom is more precious than rubies, and nothing you desire can compare with her" (Proverbs 8:4–11).

Many people have become so discouraged by what they feel, quite rightly, are conflicting and contradictory views, that they have decided to throw in the towel in the unequal struggle. Others see only the rapidity with which new ideas bloom and blossom and then fade into oblivion. Some people have been so disillusioned by attending countless seminars which professed to have the Truth for as little as $250, that they have decided they will just avoid thinking for a little while and hope that perhaps the dust will settle and the horizon will clear. My sympathies are with such people, but a word of caution is necessary. While many "truths" are being propagated and numerous "new ideas" are being peddled, we should view them all in the light of what Solomon wrote: "What has been will be again, what has been done will be done again; there is nothing new under the sun. Is there anything of which one can say, 'Look! This is something new'? It was here already, long ago; it was here before our time" (Ecclesiastes 1:9, 10).

The truth of the matter is that the new philosophies are nothing more than the old ones in modern dress, and the contemporary attitudes are strikingly similar to those demonstrated as long ago as Eden. If we can see the newness that is so attractive is not new at all, then we may be open to seeing that the truth may be at least as ancient as the things we thought were new. When it comes to the truth that God requires his people to learn and act upon, this is definitely true. Wisdom herself insisted, "The LORD possessed me at the beginning of his work, before his deeds of old; I was appointed from eternity, from the beginning, before the world began . . . . Then I was the craftsman at his side. I was filled with delight day after day, rejoicing always in his presence, rejoicing in his whole world and delighting in mankind" (Proverbs 8:22–31).

I know of few things more exciting than to discover that God used wisdom to bring the worlds into being, continues to keep them in being through his eternal wisdom, and demands that I discover this wisdom through knowing him, in order that I might function in the world he has made. It is ironic that when we consider the way in which the world so marvelously functions, whether we look at the immensity of space or the infinitesimal grandeur of the atom, that the only thing which seems to be out of step is man. The ecological balance seemed to work wonderfully well until we intervened; and having recognized the ways in which we have messed up the universe we have tried to rectify, we only discover that the corrections have sometimes been worse than the errors! This is largely attributable to man's unwillingness to submit to the ancient wisdom by which God brought all things into being and gives man the privilege of being part of the ongoing experience of God's creation.

Man's responsibility to find the wisdom by which the worlds were made, and through which they continue to exist, must surely be one of his major concerns. Some people evidence a genuine desire to come to grips with what the world is all about so that they can discover what they themselves are all about, but sadly there appear to be many people who exhibit little or no interest in such matters. Perhaps the reason for their apparent disinterest is that they feel ill-equipped to delve into such seemingly obscure areas of knowledge. There is, however, something very exciting in the passage that I just quoted.

We noted that the writer put his words in the mouth of a personification of wisdom and this has led theologians and other interested parties to indulge in long, and often heated, debates as to whether wisdom is to be regarded as a heavenly being with the Father at the time of Creation or whether it is nothing more than a literary device. Some people have seen in this passage a great statement about the Lord

Jesus Christ, of whom there are many New Testament statements which testify to his eternal nature and presence with the Father "in the beginning." Objections to this interpretation have centered around the fact that "wisdom" is female and Christ was male, and the two should not be confused! This settles the matter for some people, but there is no doubt that while the passage may not specifically refer to Christ, the New Testament writers, on a number of occasions, felt perfect liberty to draw from the imagery of Solomon's work and use these ideas to portray Christ. For example Paul wrote, concerning Christ, "He is the image of the invisible God, the firstborn over all creation. For by him all things were created: things in heaven and on earth, visible and invisible, whether thrones or powers or rulers or authorities; all things were created by him and for him. He is before all things, and in him all things hold together" (Colossians 1:15–17).

A little later in the same letter Paul described the Lord Jesus as the One "in whom are hidden all the treasures of wisdom and knowledge" (Colossians 2:3). These two Scriptures, along with many others, demonstrate conclusively that the New Testament writers not only attributed eternal being and oneness with the Father to the Son, but also declared that the wisdom of which Solomon spoke in both philosophical and practical terms was uniquely demonstrated by Christ in his earthly life. It is this fact of Christian doctrine that is so exciting and encouraging. It shows us that God not only wants to impart the knowledge of reality to us in technical and academic terms, but also desires that we should see for ourselves this wisdom in action. Rather than God being the professor of wisdom in the university of life, delivering lectures and promising stiff examinations, the fact that Christ, "who has become for us wisdom from God" (1 Corinthians 1:30), came into the world shows God to be the One who demonstrates in his own Son what he teaches in his own word. The "professor" leads the field trips, experiments with his students, and even stoops to feel their anguish, identify with their needs, and share their sorrows and joys.

The wisdom of God in Christ, therefore, becomes more than something learned from a book of sayings. It becomes a thrilling experience of studying a life in action and responding to the invitation of the living One, even the risen Christ, to open our lives to him, so that by the Holy Spirit he might enter our lives and impart his wisdom to us. With this in mind, the words of Solomon have a familiar ring: "Wisdom has built her house; she has hewn out its seven pillars. She has prepared her meat and mixed her wine; she has also set her table. She has sent out her maids, and she calls from the highest point of the city. 'Let all who are simple come in here!' she says to those who lack judgment. 'Come, eat my food and drink the wine I have mixed. Leave your simple ways and you will live; walk in the way of understanding'" (Proverbs 9:1–6). The familiar sound of these words comes from our familiarity with the words of the Lord himself when he told the parable of the banquet, where "a certain man was preparing a great banquet and invited many guests. At the time of the banquet he sent his servant to tell those who had been invited, 'Come, for everything is now ready.' But they all alike began to make excuses" (Luke 14:16–18). Christ told the parable to remind people that God, in Christ, had prepared all the blessings of the Kingdom of God for all people, but they had the responsibility to learn of his provision and then to accept the invitation to participate in the blessings. Aware as he was that people are strangely reluctant to avail themselves of all that Christ has to offer them, he made it abundantly clear that those who choose to ignore or reject the invitation to participate in the banquet will bear sole responsibility for their own spiritual loss and eternal deprivation.

Where, then, does the buck stop? Firstly, we must say that the Scripture clearly insists that every man must avail himself of the opportunities he has to learn of the ways and will of God. Failure to do so will leave him guilty before God, because ignorance is no excuse. Secondly, there is a clear statement that every man has the responsibility to decide what he will do about the things he has learned. God has made truth available, and in so doing has laid moral responsibility on each person so enlightened. To fail to learn what is learnable and to obey what is commanded is to place oneself in the position of being morally and eternally estranged from the purposes of God. There the buck stops.

NINE

Humility Comes Before Honor

The fear of the LORD teaches a man wisdom, and humility comes before honor.

Proverbs 15:33

The lot of a celebrity is not always a happy one. Because, as someone rather cynically pointed out, "a celebrity is a person who's famous for being well-known." Celebrities have to live with the recognition of their fans and the demands that their fans feel they have every right to make. As a result, some of the glamour people of our society have to live their lives in the most unglamorous ways. The Beatles used to complain that they had to eat their meals in hotel bedrooms, enter buildings through kitchens, and depart via fire escapes. It is not uncommon for celebrities to suffer having their hair cut, their clothes torn, their cars mobbed, their possessions taken as souvenirs, and their families exposed to all manner of insult and innuendo. They spend their lives being hounded, guarded, coddled, and scheduled.

On the other side of the coin, there seem to be many things about celebrity status that make a lot of people feel it is worth achieving. Not that it always takes much ability to achieve celebrity status in our modern world. Shakespeare observed, "Some men are born great, some achieve greatness, and some have greatness thrust upon them," and it appears that there are more "celebrities" who fit into Shakespeare's third category than the first two in our world.

A few days ago I was talking to a friend of mine who was a successful professional basketball player. He talked warmly about his experiences as an athlete, and he was most anxious to point out that any degree of recognizability that he has and any renown which he may possess are attributable solely to his athletic abilities and achievements. Almost ruefully he said it was ironic that, although his main claim to fame was that he could throw a ball through a hoop, other people in the community who had done much to help the needy and support the weak were unknown and unheralded. But he recognized that even though he had had fame thrust upon him for what, to him, were not very good reasons, he also acknowledged his responsibility to use his fame and honor wisely and to the greatest possible advantage for his community.

Not all celebrities have such a healthy, mature attitude. In fact, some of them seem to have gained the impression, from some strange source, that the world owes them something, and it is their right to expect the world to deliver it to them on a silver platter. Recently another well-known athlete, whose raw talents were legendary and whose promise as a superstar was phenomenal, talked about his total failure as an athlete and a man. He came up to no one's expectations, failed lamentably to play up to his potential, became estranged from his teammates, alienated from management, feuded with his coaches, and held a running battle with the press until in the end, when he should have been at the peak of his career, he quit in disgust and despair. He put it down to his inability to live with recognition and cope with the demands and rewards of sudden fame. Perhaps he would have done better if he had known and heeded Solomon's words, "The fear of the LORD teaches a man wisdom, and humility comes before honor" (Proverbs 15:33). Of course, the celebrity is not entirely to blame. The society which makes celebrities out of people who have remarkably little to offer, that society is, itself, suspect. Where are the values of a society which gladly pays a rock star, of doubtful musical ability, more for one night's performance than it will pay its President for one year's leadership? I recognize that some people will say, "Because having watched the President, we think the rock star is worth more!" But I assume that would be a political response laced with sarcasm! Solomon had trenchant words on this subject, too. "Like snow in summer or rain in harvest, honor is not fitting for a fool" (Proverbs 26:1).

The Apostle Paul would not have felt particularly comfortable honoring those whom he felt were unworthy of honor, but at the same time, he insisted that those to whom it was due should be rightly regarded. Writing to the Christians in Rome, who had their own special problems because of their station in life and the tricky situation in which they lived, he said, "Give everyone what you owe him. If you owe taxes, pay taxes; if revenues, then revenue; if respect, then respect; if honor, then honor" (Romans 13:7). This being the case, we need to seriously consider the question, "Who is worthy of honor, and to whom is respect and honor due?" Paul's answer would have been partly that the position to which a person has risen in the society, even though the society may not be Christian by any stretch of the imagination, might make him worthy of honor, because he functions as God's servant in that position. This information may indeed come as quite a shock to the official who didn't even know he was serving the Lord!

The Lord Jesus, with his remarkably different perspective from practically everyone else, pointed out to his disciples, "He that is least among you all—he is the greatest" (Luke 9:48). He was talking not so much about celebrity status on earth but greatness in the eyes of God and celebrity status in the Kingdom of God. His oft-quoted words, "The first shall be last and the last shall be first," speak to this fact of spiritual principle so often ignored. Even in the spiritual realm, we are in danger of making our own celebrities out of those whose gifts and charisma give them front-line positions and spotlight coverage, instead of heeding the words of the Master, "Whoever wants to become great among you must be your servant, and whoever wants to be first must be slave of all" (Mark 10:43, 44).

It was this that Solomon had in mind when he wrote, "Humility comes before honor." There are two ways of looking at this proverb. Firstly, it can mean that humility is more valuable than honor; and secondly, real honor will come only to the truly humble. There is a sense in which they are both true and cannot be true without each other. In God's reckoning, there obviously is a principle of evaluation which differs markedly from human standards. As Paul said to the Corinthian Christians, "Brothers, think of what you were when you were called. Not many of you were of noble birth. But God chose the foolish things of the world to shame the wise, and the despised things—and the things that are not—to nullify the things that are" (1 Corinthians 1:26–28). To the society of which we are a part, that which has attained celebrity status may be rated very poorly in the divine reckoning, and that which is unknown may be of prime importance in terms of eternal issues and divine perspectives.

It is God's intention that man should see himself in proper perspective so that he will be humbled by what he is and, instead of blowing his own trumpet and beating his own drum, he might come to the Father and ask for forgiveness and seek to be blessed by God. The truly honorable person in God's book is the humbly repentant one, who has been honored as a child of God and an heir of Christ, a member of the Kingdom of God and a recipient of eternal life. When we understand this, we will grasp what Peter meant when he wrote to the early believer, "Clothe yourselves with humility toward one another, because, 'God opposes the proud but gives grace to the humble.' Humble yourselves, therefore, under God's might hand, that He may lift you up in due time" (1 Peter 5:5, 6). But to do this is not as easy as would at first appear. The reason that we do experience difficulty is that our standards of value differ so greatly from God's standards. In our modern society we applaud winners and tend to dismiss losers. This means that we encourage aggressiveness and assertiveness, which we feel are in total opposition to humbleness. Our idea of humbleness is to be passive and quiet, never to initiate anything, never to challenge anybody. We have been taught that the world is out there to be won, and it will be the strong who win and the weak will go to the wall. "Weak" and "humble" have become synonymous in much of contemporary secular thought, and the idea of being humble is, therefore, as unpalatable as being a "loser" and as unattractive as being a second-rate citizen.

A moment's thought, however, will show that not all the great winners of recent years turned out to be such great winners after all. Many won prizes and defeated opponents, challenged the status quo and overcame obstacles, but at the same time they faded into oblivion, their faces were no longer recognized, and some of them even allowed American Express to advertise the fact in their commercials! Many were successes in one area, but terrible failures in others.

Some were able to rout political opposition, but were helpless in the grip of vice. Many lived powerfully, but died ignominiously. Some had life by the tail until the tail wrapped around them and held them helpless in its grip.

There is a great need for us to understand what it means to be humble and why humility is so necessary. The only place I know to start understanding the subject is in the Word of God. When we do this, we promptly escape the perspectives of humans and see from the slant of heaven, the view of God.

Some years ago a veteran missionary was staying in my home. During his stay, a particularly precocious young student in a nearby Bible School asked to speak to my friend. He delivered a long lecture to the missionary on the subject of his own attributes and excellences and came to a crashing climax with the immortal words, "My father thinks that for me to serve God as a missionary would be a total waste." The veteran looked up slowly and with a steady, quiet voice said, "So much for your father's view of God. Now let me tell you God's view of your father." It is God's view of man that is so largely misunderstood, because man likes to spend time expressing his view of God instead of taking time to learn God's view of man. To be reminded that "The eyes of the LORD are everywhere, keeping watch on the wicked and the good" (Proverbs 15:3) is to be alerted to the possibility of his watching us. To know that "Death and destruction lie open before the LORD—how much more the hearts of men?" (Proverbs 15:11) is to remember that he not only watches, but that he sees more than we think he can see. Like the satellite moving silently through the heavens, watching the moves of the enemy so carefully that its cameras can record the numbers on the trucks, the state of the harvest, the presence of underground activity, and the movement of the smallest item, so the eyes of the Lord search the minutest details of the heart of man.

But he not only sees, he also evaluates: "The LORD detests the sacrifice of the wicked, but the prayer of the upright pleases him. The LORD detests the way of the wicked but he loves those who pursue righteousness" (Proverbs 15:8, 9). Coupled with his all-seeing and carefully evaluating oversight of the human race, there is a further factor which should never be overlooked. Namely his moral rectitude and commitment to doing that which is right in response to man's actions. "The LORD detests all the proud of heart. Be sure of this: They will not go unpunished" (Proverbs 16:5). Thoughts like these, which turn our attention to the divine perspective, are sobering; perhaps that is why we don't think about them very often! There are two possible reactions to this revelation of God's view. First, we can reject it and assure ourselves it is meaningless and irrelevant. Secondly, we can believe it and wonder what to do about it.

To be humble is to be realistic. It is to look at myself from the vantage point of heaven and to evaluate myself by the criteria of eternity. To see myself not as I think I am, not as my supporters tell me I am, not even as those who love me insist I am, but simply as God knows I am. To see myself like this is to be realistic and to be humble. It may mean divorcing myself from the advice of those who tell me only what they think I want to hear. It may mean that I no longer associate solely with those whose objectives are exactly the same as mine. It most certainly does mean that I place myself before the scrutinizing gaze of Scripture and agree with God's evaluation of me.

It is because the Word of God is so uncompromising and uncomplimentary that many people will not read it. They don't say they don't read it because they dislike what it says about them, they prefer to raise objections about its validity and question its authenticity! But the Word stands as a silent witness to that which is true about their lives, whether or not they admit it.

To be caught up with my own ambitions and to be enamored with my own importance may quite possibly lead me through various stages to the spotlight of recognition and the status of celebrity. But there is a sad side to this kind of endeavor, because the person so orientated has a very small world in which to live and small universe to conquer. Their world is no greater than the limits of their understanding, and the horizons of their universe stretch no further than the limits of their ambition. Many a success story has a failure ending for no other reason than the success gained was so limited, and when gained, left the winner with a transient thrill of victory, which gradually paled into something suspiciously like the emptiness of defeat.

The heavenly perspective, however, never leaves a person with a sense of having achieved all there is to achieve. Neither does it allow anyone to assume that they have done all there is to do. On the contrary, the more the person on earth becomes aware of his place in the vastness of eternity and the purpose of God, the more he sees himself not as a great success in a very small field, but as part of a vast whole which will come to consummation through the power of God. This is, of course, very humbling but again extremely realistic.

The person unwilling or unable to see himself in such a framework wrestles with one of the most dangerous problems known to man—the problem of pride. Wrapped up in his own schemes, seeking nothing greater than his own success, he places his puniness in the place of God's greatness and substitutes his plastic universe for the wholeness of that which God has made. To do this is to pay God the ultimate insult, and that is why, "The LORD tears down the proud man's house, but he keeps the widow's boundaries intact" (Proverbs 15:25). But there is also the reminder that, "a man's pride brings him low, but a man of lowly spirit gains honor" (Proverbs 29:23).

There are many other things in Scripture which, when believed, bring men and women to a humble attitude before their God. The recognition that God knows and understands their hearts, the understanding that he evaluates their innermost thoughts and intentions, the discovery of the smallness of their lives in the immensity of the universe, and the finiteness of their being in the grandeur of eternity, all lead to shamefaced admission of guilt and pride, which in itself leads to forgiveness and reconciliation to God. But it also leads to honor. True, real honor, because as we saw at the beginning of this chapter, "Humility comes before honor." One of the verses I learned in early days through the teaching of my parents was, "Those who honor me I will honor, but those who despise me will be disdained" (1 Samuel 2:30). They taught me this verse from childhood, because they knew that I was born to live in a world that would offer me many honors and promise me many prizes. Many of them would be noble and good, but others would be ignoble and evil. In order that I might have a principle to work by, they reminded me of God's promise that if I would seek to honor him, he would see that I got my fair share of honor. They also reminded me that if I set out to honor myself, I was on my own in a big cold world full of people seeking their own honor.

The promise that God will honor those who honor him by humbly submitting to his control of their lives is one of the most precious things mankind can possibly discover.

A tremendous burden rests on those who seek honor as a result of their own efforts based on their own abilities. They have to live in a competitive world, full of people looking for the same honors.

They also have to live with themselves, knowing deep in their hearts that some of the things in their honor-studded lives are less than honorable. They also have to confront the realities of eternity sometime when the transient nature of their honors will be demonstrated, and the fact of their inattention to lasting issues may become apparent.

The person who seeks only to humbly live before his God and serve him through the enabling power of the Holy Spirit, does not have to compete, he never need pretend, he has nothing to cover up, and he has no fears about missing out when the honors are handed out, because God, himself, has promised honor to the ones who honor him.

Those who live in the consciousness of this kind of honor move through life exuding confidence. Not self-confidence, which obviously cannot exist alongside a humble spirit, but the confidence that comes from knowing that, weak and sinful though they may be, they have been accepted and forgiven, restored and recycled, and now from that position of strength, they move calmly and confidently into whatever lies ahead. Solomon said it thus: "He who fears the LORD has a secure fortress, and for his children it will be a refuge" (Proverbs 14:26). This sense of well-being that comes through being honored by God is recognized and enjoyed even in the most difficult circumstances. In my work as a pastor, I have innumerable opportunities to see the truth of Solomon's words work out in practice: "When calamity comes, the wicked are brought down, but even in death the righteous have a refuge" (Proverbs 14:32). You will, of course, have noticed the stark realism of the words "When calamity comes. . . ." Solomon did not evade the issue by saying "If calamity comes . . . ", neither did he give the false impression that once we have committed ourselves to the Lord, instant exemption from calamity is promised. The believer, honored through humility, knows that his honor will be demonstrated and his humility tested in the way he handles the kind of calamities other people are called to face and are required to handle.

Another side product of the promise of honor is that, in addition to a sense of confidence, the believer exhibits a beautiful sense of cheerfulness: "A happy heart makes the face cheerful, but heartache crushes the spirit" (Proverbs 15:13). The person who anticipates the blessing of God has every reason to be cheerful. Life holds no terrors for him, because he has long ago determined that his course shall be a humble walk with God, wherever He leads. Death holds no mysteries for him either, because he has the assurance of the strong refuge "even in death." With a sense of adequacy for life and the assurance of victory in death, the believer can afford to be cheerful. Unfortunately, this is not always exemplified in Christian walk and demeanor, but the understanding of the reasons for a cheerful heart should be carefully taught to those who don't know about it and should be strongly reiterated to those who know but have chosen to forget. The reason that the demonstration of cheerfulness is so important is that a lot of people need to see real joy and be exposed to the reasons for such joy. "A cheerful look brings joy to the heart, and good news gives health to the bones"(Proverbs 15: 30).

Finally, the person who lives in harmony with the Lord will demonstrate a charitable life-style. I have discovered that many people are looking for encouragement because they get so little of it. This morning, after I had preached a third morning service, a young lady waited quite a long time to talk to me, as a number of others were also claiming my attention. When, eventually, I was able to turn to her, I remembered that she had been to see me during the week and I had been able to spend an hour with her, not dealing with any great problems, but mainly listening to what she had to say and then making one or two simple suggestions. I wondered what had gone wrong when I saw her there, but she just wanted to thank me for the time I had given her and the advice I had shared with her. I tried to assure her, "It was nothing. It was my pleasure!" but she refused to allow me to say it. "You don't know what it meant to me to have you listen to me and to be shown that you cared. I know you're busy and I know that you pastor a large church, so I thought you would not have time for me and when I discovered you had, it was such an encouragement to me that I was ready to take your advice and do what you recommended." My mind went immediately to Solomon's words, "A man finds joy in giving an apt reply, and how good is a timely word!" (Proverbs 15:23). People need words sometimes and more tangible evidences of our charity other times. When we are no longer living to produce and preserve our own honor but have centered our desires in his honor, we will have time to do for people what they need, as well as listen to them and speak a timely word to them. "A generous man will himself be blessed, for he shares his food with the poor" (Proverbs 22:9).

Let us heed the words of the wise man about our misplaced ambitions and misguided objectives, and let us settle to be nothing more and nothing less than God's humble servants, satisfied to be honored by him in his own time and in his own way. To live any other way is to live out of step with eternity and out of harmony with God. To be anything else is to be something considerably less than a person who has discovered how to live successfully.

TEN

Life's Tensions

*A man cannot be established through
wickedness, but the righteous cannot be
uprooted. . . . A righteous man cares for
the needs of his animal, but the kindest
acts of the wicked are cruel. . . . He who
guards his lips guards his soul, but he who
speaks rashly will come to ruin.*

Proverbs 12:3, 10; 13:3

We have to live with tension. In fact, we cannot
live without it! Muscles go flabby without the tension
of regular use, minds become sterile without the
challenge of new ideas, and character degenerates
into selfishness when ease and comfort become the
dominant themes of existence.

This is true not only for individuals, but also for
societies. When countries face a common enemy
they band together and strain united endeavors to
overcome that which threatens them. This was certainly the case in England during the days of the
infamous "Blitz." The people of London showed remarkable fortitude and resilience as night after night

they headed for the underground shelters, ready for the fearsome pounding of their city which they had grown to expect. The manner in which they suffered hardship, the way in which they gave of themselves for each other, and the spirit with which they faced apparently insuperable odds were incredible. No wonder Churchill said, "Let us brace ourselves to our duty and so bear ourselves, that if the British Commonwealth and Empire lasts for a thousand years, men will still say, 'This was their finest hour!' " Many people who know Britain feel that, so far, Churchill was right and only time will show whether he was completely right.

Not all tensions that people experience produce strength of character and body. Some people, rather than growing through their tension experiences, are destroyed by them. Countless people seeking counsel and comfort have related to me, in the quietness of my study, the details of their lives. I am constantly amazed at the problems some people face and the degree of tension to which some are subjected. Many are the stories of incredible courage and triumph I have heard, but sadly many are the stories of defeat and destruction I have been told. It is the way tensions are handled that determines whether we grow through them or are ground into the dust by them.

The area of greatest potential triumph or defeat is the area of moral tension, but it is a sad reflection on our modern society that this is not always understood or accepted. The tensions that arise from social impoverishment, physical infirmity, marital discord, family disintegration, financial obligations, or personal expectations are readily understood, because they are clearly recognizable. The tensions of not being able to pay the rent, or handle the kids, or cope with study, or satisfy the boss, or please the wife are plain to see and relatively easy to understand. But when we get into the realm of moral tension, everything is not quite so clear-cut. Part of the reason for this is some people do not accept the premise that there are moral absolutes, that such things as right and wrong exist, and others, while they accept that these exist, do not regard them as sufficiently important to require their attention or adherence.

Perhaps the most troublesome aspect of the contemporary attitude is that many people are comfortable with the position that if something feels and seems right to them, they should go ahead with it, provided nobody else is going to be hurt by their action. This throws the door open for all manner of abuse, because it leads us back to the old days of the judges when, "In those days Israel had no king; everyone did as he saw fit" (Judges 21:25).

Enormous problems inevitably arise in any society which runs on the basis of everyone being free, in fact, having the "inalienable right" to do as he sees fit. Without any ultimate understanding of what is right or wrong, confusion must result. The current debates on homosexuality and abortion are two obvious examples. If we argue from the premise that everyone has the right to do what they think is suitable, there is no hope of a solution. The expectant mother may insist on the right to do whatever she thinks fit with her own body, but the father may insist on his right to see his child born; and some people believe the unborn child has some rights of his own, even though nobody can hear from him what they are. The rights of everyone in such a case cannot be acceded to, nor can everyone be free to do what they think fit, while allowing everyone else the right to do the same thing.

Homosexuals, who feel they have the right to indulge in their "sexual preference," can make a powerful case if everybody is free to do what they see fit, but they run into problems when they allow the same right to everybody else. Some people find overt homosexual activity distasteful, others feel that their children may be adversely affected by exposure to homosexuals, and others are convinced that it is deviant behavior which cannot and must not be tolerated. How can all these people be left free to do what they feel is fit? Society cannot operate on this basis. It never has and it never will.

The biblical position when adhered to does not place society in the predicament we have just outlined. Scripture takes bold stands on issues and states unequivocally that right and wrong coexist, and man is to live in the tension of that coexistence. It is this tension which, in many ways, is the most dangerous and challenging for the human race. Solomon, when he wrote his Proverbs, was very much aware of the conflict between right and wrong and had much to say about the choices to be made in the moral arena.

His oft-repeated use of the words "righteous" and "wicked" to describe the attitudes and life-styles of certain people need to be studied carefully.

Before we turn our attention to the specific statements he made in the Proverbs, it might be useful for us to outline the broad teaching of Scripture on the subjects of righteousness and wickedness. The Apostle John wrote, with characteristic solemnity, about the world condition, "We know that we are the children of God, and that the whole world is under the control of the evil one" (1 John 5:19). The Lord Jesus demonstrated his firm belief in such an "evil one," when he explained the parable of the sower: "When anyone hears the message about the Kingdom and does not understand it, the evil one comes and snatches away what was sown in his heart" (Matthew 13:19). He went even further when, in scathing rebuke to the Pharisees who had the idea that personal sanctity was the result of careful abstinence from external evil, he said, "What comes out of a man is what makes him 'unclean.' For from within [out of men's hearts] come evil thoughts, sexual immorality, theft, murder, adultery, greed, malice, deceit, lewdness, envy, slander, arrogance, and folly. All these evils come from inside and make a man 'unclean' " (Mark 7:20–22).

The person who wants to seriously consider living rightly in this world, must bear in mind what the Scripture teaches about the world in which he lives. It is under the dominating power of an evil being, who being in total opposition to God and his Son, uses considerable powers to deflect people from the Truth and to hinder their experience of the Truth. Should they become exposed to the Truth, he does not give up, but does all he can to distract them in their examination of the Truth. The evil one finds an ally in the human heart, which has a great propensity for sin and a troublesome affinity to evil. In fact, human beings live in a world which is overruled by a being whose evil is legendary and where wickedness is rife. They are exposed to all manner of evil temptations to which they are disconcertingly vulnerable. A picture that hardly fits in with the optimistic, humanistic view to which we are so often exposed, for no apparent reason, in our present society!

On the other hand, the Scriptures have some extremely positive things to say to those who are prepared to accept the negative things we have just outlined. In total contrast to the control of the evil one in the world, there is the advent of the Christ into the same world. The cataclysmic confrontation in the wilderness some two thousand years ago showed that Jesus was more than a match for the evil one, who from that day on knew his days were numbered, but he had to wait another three years before his total humiliation on Calvary. The trump card of the evil one is death, and to his intense delight he was able to see his greatest enemy go down into death, even the death of a cross. But what he didn't know was that this was all part of a divine plan to show that God, in Christ, could beat the evil one at his own game, and beat him He did, through the glorious

Resurrection. This Resurrection becomes the cornerstone of man's experience. When he realizes the degree to which he has been influenced by the evil one in the evil world through the response of his evil heart, he has no problem recognizing the immensity of his own sin and the necessity for forgiveness through the death of Christ. But what he may not realize, having been forgiven, is that he is now called to live a new life in the old world. When he does realize this, he will probably be confronted with many disconcerting situations which he feels totally incapable of handling, but there is hope for the one who would live rightly before his God and Savior. This hope is in the Risen Christ who, himself, comes into the life of the redeemed sinner to give him the power to obey and the will to triumph. It was the Apostle John who stated with admirable clarity, "The one who is in you is greater than the one who is in the world" (1 John 4:4).

The tension of the believer, therefore, is monumental. It is the tension of being in a world and system to which he belongs and yet doesn't belong at the same time. Like spacemen in a capsule orbiting the earth or divers in a bell submerged beneath the ocean, he is functioning in an environment to which he does not really belong. His presence there is real and important, but he maintains his position there through his contact with outside sources. The position of the believer in the world makes it imperative that he should be constantly in touch, through his built-in support systems, with the power of God as he lives for God in an environment which is not only hostile to God, but also hazardous to his own spiritual and moral well-being.

Some people decide the struggle is too great and the tensions are too demanding, so they either throw in their lot with the world which lives in constant conflict with their God, or they try to live for their God by isolation from their world. Neither option is offered to the believer, as both the example and the words of our Lord clearly demonstrate.

As the "friend of sinners," he was constantly in contact with all types of people, fully conversant with their life-styles, totally concerned about their needs, yet never identified with their sin. His opponents, failing to understand his remarkable ability to live in the tension between good and evil without identifying himself totally or completely isolating himself, criticized him viciously, yet fell into the trap of their own making. To them, he was associating with sinners and, therefore, was partaking of their sin. While, because they were disassociating with sinners, they were keeping themselves free from sin. In fact, he was in touch with sinners yet sinless himself, while they were not in touch with sinners, yet falling into all manner of sin themselves.

As we have seen, the Hebrew writers were particularly fond of a poetic form called parallelism, where ideas were set in marked contrast to each other. This type of writing was used by Solomon with great effect when he talked about the difference between wickedness and goodness, and the people who practiced both, whom he called the "wicked" and the "righteous." For instance, "A man cannot be established through wickedness, but the righteous cannot be uprooted" (Proverbs 12:3), or "Wicked men are overthrown and are no more, but the house of the righteous stands firm" (Proverbs 12:7). Once we have accepted the fact of the existence of good and evil in our world and the necessity to live rightly in a world that is prone to live wrongly, it is helpful for us to compare the alternative life-styles and attitudes of the wicked and the righteous. Verses like those quoted above give much food for thought, because they confront us in vivid language with the greatness of the choices to be made and the vastness of the consequences of such choices.

At the back of all behavior patterns lies a philosophy of life. Scripture states very clearly that unless the philosophy comes from the mind of God and the life-style is built on the truth of God, there is no hope of life being lived correctly. At this point, the battle is joined and the decisions are made. "He who scorns instruction will pay for it, but he who respects a command is rewarded" (Proverbs 13:13). There are those who openly despise the Word of God, while others, not quite so forthright, simply ignore it. Left without any absolute standards for behavior, they are adrift on a sea full of treacherous currents, and as Solomon said, "They will pay for it."

It is a simple fact of life that for many years in the western world much of our social morality has been derived from scriptural principle, and so many people have adhered to principles of truth without knowing that was what they were doing. In some cases, people who have despised the Word of God have unwittingly obeyed it, because they lived by the accepted norm, which they did not realize was a biblical principle. But those days are going, if they have not already gone. In recent years, there has been such an erosion of public confidence in the Word of God, and such a massive substituting of secular dogma for the truth of God, that even "Christian" societies have placed considerable distance between themselves and that which is remotely Christian. This makes the necessity for decision concerning the basis of a philosophy of life more urgent. But it also draws the lines of demarcation more clearly, and soon there will be no opportunity for vague uncommitted attitudes, because everyone will have to decide whether their approach is fundamentally secular or spiritual, and whether they will build on foundations of divine demand or contemporary caprice.

The choices made at this level become clearly apparent at many other levels. In the area of integrity, for instance, the differences are great: "The plans of the righteous are just, but the advice of the wicked is deceitful" (Proverbs 12:5). To do business with a man committed to doing what is right according to God's standards of rightness is a much less taxing experience than doing the same kind of business with a man whose only interest is his own gain. The former can reasonably be expected to demonstrate honesty and integrity, but the latter may need watching like a hawk. This statement is not to be interpreted as saying that the only honest business-men are believers, or even that all believers are scrupulously honest. But it does say that if a business-man does not base his principles of business on an ethic greater than that which prevails in a less than perfect world, there is every chance that he may be less than honest in what he says and less than trans-parent in why he says it.

Conversation is another area in which the differ-ence of life, philosophy, and choice is readily recog-nizable. The power of words to harm or heal is not always appreciated. The ability of words to galvan-ize, to motivate, to judge, to condemn, to relieve, or to educate is much greater than we normally realize. But when we consider that the words of our mouths are the reflections of our thoughts, intentions, and attitudes, words take on a major new significance. Jesus said, "Out of the overflow of the heart the mouth speaks" (Matthew 12:34), and Solomon added the thought-provoking words, "The tongue has the power of life and death" (Proverbs 18:21).

Examples of the contrasting use of words are too numerous to repeat, but the following sample will suffice to show how different is the talk of the righ-teous man and the wicked man, and how great is the gulf between what is accomplished by words of truth and words of strife. "With his mouth the godless de-stroys his neighbor, but through knowledge the righteous escape" (Proverbs 11:9); "A gossip betrays a confidence, but a trustworthy man keeps a secret" (Proverbs 11:13); "The words of the wicked lie in wait for blood, but the speech of the upright rescues them" (Proverbs 12:6); "An evil man is trapped by his sinful talk, but a righteous man escapes trouble" (Proverbs 12:13); "A truthful witness gives honest testimony, but a false witness tells lies. Reckless words pierce like a sword, but the tongue of the wise brings healing. Truthful lips endure forever, but a lying tongue lasts only a moment" (Proverbs 12:17–19); "He who guards his lips guards his soul, but he who speaks rashly will come to ruin" (Proverbs 13:3).

Proverbs has much to say on the vital subject of personal relationships. Like other areas of human experience, these, too, are the products of decisions. Either we choose to obey God in our attitudes to people, or we decide to do that which is right in our own eyes towards our neighbors. There is sufficient evidence in our world at the present to show that far too many people regard other people, at worst, as objects of hatred and ridicule and, at best, as the means of personal advancement. The strong insistence of Scripture that we are related through our Creator to each other, that we are all made in the image of God, and that in Christ there is common brotherhood, demands that people behave in a special way to each other. But the rejection of these truths leaves the door open to all manner of abuse. The unusual words, "A righteous man cares for the needs of his animal, but the kindest acts of the wicked are cruel" (Proverbs 12:10), are designed not so much to convey the thought that believers are all animal lovers and all animal lovers are believers, but rather that the righteous feel more compassion for their animals than the wicked feel for people. This is easily illustrated from the astounding fact that people will spend lavishly on dog food and give nothing for famine relief and will weep copiously over the death of a canary without sharing the slightest concern for the demise of an innocent infant in a foreign war. The cruelty of the sophisticated person is seen not so much in overt acts of violence and torture, as in callous indifference to human need and sometimes even hostile attitudes to those who suffer. It is not uncommon to hear people who have never suffered a moment's hardship in their whole life charging the less fortunate with all types of wickedness, when in actuality the wickedness is more often in evidence on the lips of the critics than in the lives of those being criticized. Such critics of poor people have paid little regard to such traumatic and unavoidable circumstances as those Solomon mentioned: "A poor man's field may produce abundant food, but injustice sweeps it away" (Proverbs 13:23). Before succumbing to sinful attitudes that poison human relationships and demonstrate the reality of our own sinfulness, we should take to heart the words, "He who despises his neighbor sins, but blessed is he who is kind to the needy" (Proverbs 14:21), and we should carefully study the even more pointed statement, "He who oppresses the poor shows contempt for their Maker, but whoever is kind to the needy honors God" (Proverbs 14:31).

Having accepted the fact that there are tensions of rightness and wrongness in our world, and having come to the decision that we wish to yield ourselves to the right and live righteously before God in the power of his risen Son, we should take time out to carefully evaluate our intentions, our words, and our relationships. Great differences exist in the life-styles of those who live according to different principles, and there is no more accurate measure of the reality of a person's commitment than the examination of his output in these areas.

Before concluding this chapter, it might be good to list some of the ingredients necessary for us to live rightly in the tension between good and evil. They are as follows:

1. Awareness of good and evil
2. Boldness in identifying good and evil
3. Carefulness in recognizing good and evil
4. Decisiveness in choosing good or evil
5. Effectiveness in doing good, not evil
6. Faithfulness in maintaining good rather than evil

Finally, let me remind you of the different prospects awaiting those who choose one way or the other. "The light of the righteous shines brightly, but the lamp of the wicked is snuffed out" (Proverbs 13:9).

Direction for a closer and more personal walk with God

____ **GOD WITHIN by Jean T. Dibden**
An example for Christians who wish to develop a keener awareness of God's guidance on a day-to-day basis as this listener has done.   paper $1.50

____ **THE MASTER PLAN OF EVANGELISM**
by Robert E. Coleman
Methods and concepts of evangelism based on the scriptural pattern of Jesus and His disciples.
                                                   paper $1.95

____ **THE CHRISTIAN'S SECRET OF A HAPPY LIFE**
by Hannah Whitall Smith
A well-known classic on happiness and the Christian life.   paper $2.25

____ **THE PRACTICE OF THE PRESENCE OF GOD**
by Brother Lawrence
The intimate account of how one man lived his daily life with God.   paper $1.7